The
CARE AND
FEEDING
of YOUR
CHI

The
CARE AND
FEEDING
of YOUR
CHI

Feng Shui for Your Body

SKYE ALEXANDER

FAIR WINDS
PRESS
GLOUCESTER, MASSACHUSETTS

Text © 2004 Skye Alexander

First published in the USA in 2004 by
Fair Winds Press
33 Commercial Street
Gloucester, MA 01930

08 07 06 05 04   2 3 4 5

ISBN 1-59233-078-9

Library of Congress Cataloging-in-Publication Data available

Cover and book design by Laura Herrmann Design
Cover illustration by Elizabeth Cornaro

Printed and bound in Canada

*The information in this book is for educational purposes only. It is not
intended to replace the advice of a physician or medical practitioner.*

Dedication

To Laurie and Matt

Contents

INTRODUCTION

Chi exists everywhere, in every living thing—even in things most people wouldn't consider animate, such as our homes, the land, and the sky. It is the life force or vital energy of the universe, the Divine breath or spirit that quickens matter. Without chi, life as we know it could not exist.

The concept of chi originates in ancient Chinese philosophy. Similar ideas can be found in other Eastern spiritual and medical traditions as well as in Western esoteric teachings and holistic healing concepts, where chi goes by names such as *prana, orgone, ki, reiki,* and *vis medicatrix naturae.*

Dowsers and feng shui practitioners map chi that flows through the land. Astrologers chart the cosmic chi generated by celestial and metaphysical forces. According to Taoism, one of China's major spiritual traditions and the philosophy that underlies feng shui, everything in our universe is interconnected—human life is affected by the energies of the earth and sky, and in turn our energies affect the cosmos. "Tao is a process and a principle linking man with the Universe," explains Sarah Rossbach in her book *Interior Design with Feng Shui*. In order to be happy and healthy, we must learn to live in harmony with nature and our environment, and with the universal energies that are present all around us in the heavens and the earth.

Feng Shui for the Body

The goal of feng shui is to manipulate chi so that it flows through an environment in a balanced, unhampered manner. To accomplish this objective, feng shui practitioners employ a variety of techniques known as "cures" that are both practical and esoteric. Some of the most common cures include arranging furniture in comfortable configurations, clearing away clutter, and balancing yin and yang forces through the use of plants, minerals, color, light, sound, and so on.

The goal of many holistic healing modalities is to manipulate chi so that it flows through the body in a balanced, unhampered manner. To accomplish this objective, healers employ a variety of techniques or cures, both practical and esoteric, to create a body-mind-spirit synergy. Some of the most common cures include diet, exercise, relaxation, spiritual practice, mental discipline, and balancing yin and yang forces through the use of plants, minerals, color, light, and sound.

In both feng shui and holistic healing, the mind is the most important factor. Your intention and attitude influence the success or failure of whatever physical practices you implement. Both feng shui and holistic healing consider the nonphysical realms as well as the physical one, and work on many levels, visible and invisible, to create well-being. Therefore, the tips and techniques in this book range from very basic, obvious physical recommendations—get enough sleep, eat right, and exercise regularly—to esoteric and metaphysical suggestions—practice acceptance, live in the moment, pray, enjoy a rainbow.

How to Use This Book

To write about chi without discussing Chinese medicine would be like writing about the gasoline engine without mentioning its importance to automobiles. But this is not a book about Chinese medicine, even though some of the remedies and theories included here are rooted in Chinese healing traditions. Rather, it is a collection of ideas and techniques gleaned from a variety of sources, cultures, and systems—some ancient, some modern—that can help you strengthen the life force within you in order to enhance your health, happiness, and personal growth.

In this book, East meets West. I've attempted to present some information about Eastern and Western holistic healing modalities in a practical, accessible way, as well as some concepts drawn from both Eastern and Western mysticism. Sometimes these ideas agree and overlap; other times they diverge. For instance, Chinese medicine does not view the organs of the body and their functions the same way as Western medicine. Chinese medicine and Western herbalism use different plants for treating ailments. Instead of debating which line of thought is "better" or "right," I recommend that you try what intrigues you, study more about therapies that sound interesting, and discover for yourself which ones suit you best.

Part One explains the nature of chi and how this life force operates in our bodies and in our world. I also discuss various complementary healing concepts and practices in this section. Part Two offers hundreds of tips and techniques for healing chi, in yourself and your environment. These tips include things you can do to care for your body as well as ways to use your mind to promote well-being, balance your emotions, and connect with your essential self or spirit. Because health and happiness also depend on the presence of chi in the environment, Chapter 7 offers techniques for rectifying chi imbalances in your home, workplace, and world.

Although I've grouped these tips into four categories—body, mind and emotions, spirit, and environment—it's important to remember that true health requires a balance and unity of body, mind, and spirit. Attitude and lifestyle play major roles in well-being, therefore many of the ideas presented in Part Two encourage you to take care of yourself psychologically as well as physically. As you become more aware of how chi operates in your life, you'll develop a greater respect for the magic and power of the universe and a deeper understanding of your place in it.

For the most part, the exercises included in this book are gentle and easy enough for most people to perform. Use common sense and don't push yourself. Likewise, the holistic healing suggestions and remedies given here are widely used and safe for most individuals. Because everyone is unique, however, some of these treatments may be more suitable for you than others. To be safe, consult your physician if you have questions or before trying anything you aren't certain about.

PART
ONE

What Is CHI?

*h*ere in the West, chi (pronounced *chee*) is still a mystery to most people. The Chinese, however, have been studying, cultivating, manipulating, and working with chi for three thousand years in order to promote health, prosperity, and happiness. Their system of medicine and their martial arts revolve around chi. They base their architecture, roads, and city planning—even their cemeteries—on the movement of chi through the environment.

Chi can't be categorized as animal, vegetable, or mineral. It isn't a gas, liquid, or solid. You can't perceive chi with your five ordinary senses—it is invisible, silent, weightless, odorless, and tasteless. Yet chi permeates everything: the earth, the atmosphere, our homes, our bodies.

Chi, sometimes spelled *qi*, is the Chinese word for the vital energy that animates all things. In India, this energy is called *prana*. Biologist and psychiatrist Wilhelm Reich referred to it as *orgone*. Some metaphysicians might relate it to spirit. *Star Wars* fans could think of it as The Force. Whatever you choose to call it, chi is the fundamental, dynamic, creative energy of the universe, without which life as we know it would not exist.

Chi and Health

During the last quarter century, a "cultural revolution" of sorts has been taking place as East meets West. Eastern medicine, philosophy, and spirituality have infiltrated the West and profoundly influenced the way we perceive the world. Before 1975, for instance, only a handful of Americans had been treated by acupuncturists. Today, more than 15,000 licensed acupuncturists are operating in the U.S. Many natural food stores sell Chinese herbs, and acupuncture is performed at some major hospitals, including Beth Israel Deaconess in Boston. My dentist even gives patients the option of being numbed by acupuncture instead of novocaine.

Maintaining healthy chi is the principal concern of Chinese medicine. Practitioners of Eastern medicine believe that physical problems arise when chi becomes blocked, weakened, or doesn't move properly through the body. Acupuncturists, for example, insert needles into areas where energetic blockages occur to release chi and allow it to flow smoothly— it's a bit like unclogging a pipe so water can run freely through it again.

According to Chinese medical philosophy (and many other forms of holistic medicine), our physical bodies comprise only part of our overall health. Several other "subtle" bodies, which consist of energetic vibrations but no dense material, surround and permeate the physical one. When photographed with special types of equipment or when viewed by intuitive individuals, these subtle bodies resemble layers of colored lights rippling all around the physical form. These bodies are usually called the etheric, emotional, astral, mental, and causal bodies (in order, moving outward from the physical), each level being of a finer substance and a higher vibration than the preceding one. The term "aura" is often used in connection with the etheric body.

Holistic medicine holds that disease begins in these subtle energy bodies and only becomes apparent in the physical body during the later, more advanced stages. Therefore, the objective is to heal imbalances *before* they reach the physical stage when problems are more established and difficult to remedy. Because your thoughts and emotions affect the condition of these bodies, they can have a profound impact on your health (I'll talk more about this in Chapter 3).

Chi exists in the universe as an enlivening force. According to Chinese medicine, it flows into the subtle bodies first, then enters the physical one through the 350 acupuncture points, which serve as portals into an energetic network of channels called *meridians* that run up and down the physical body. These meridians are invisible conduits that carry chi from head to foot, distributing life-giving energy to every cell. Twelve major meridians dotted with dozens of entry points traverse the physical body, like rivers with a series of gates or vortices positioned at strategic spots. When a blockage occurs in a meridian, an acupuncturist opens a "gate" by inserting a hair-thin needle into the appropriate point, thereby stimulating the flow of chi once more.

Chi moves constantly through the body—when it stops, life ceases. It continually ascends and descends, enters and leaves, traveling through the system of meridians and the organs. According to Chinese medicine, chi circulates in a cyclic pattern—at different times of the day it reaches its maximum flow in one or another of the organs. In diagnosing and treating disease, it's important to take these time periods into consideration.

One of the ways chi travels about in our bodies is via the blood. (Don't confuse the meridians with the veins and arteries, however.) From the perspective of Chinese medicine, chi and the blood enjoy an interdependent relationship. Chi is the force that circulates the blood, while the blood nourishes the chi. A Chinese saying from Tom Williams, PhD.'s, *The Complete Illustrated Guide to Chinese Medicine*, explains it this way: "Chi is the commander of the blood, and blood is the mother of chi."[i]

We inherit "original" chi from our parents. We also acquire chi from the air we breathe and from the food we eat. External factors in the environment, as well as our emotions, thoughts, and lifestyles, affect the condition of our personal chi. By engaging in beneficial practices—such as those suggested in Part Two of this book—you can nourish your chi to enhance your health and happiness.

Chi and Fitness

In recent years, yoga, tai chi, and chi kung (also spelled *qigong*) have migrated from the East and taken root in Western soil. These ancient practices, as well as many of the martial arts, share a common denominator: They all regulate and nurture the body's chi.

More than mere physical exercises, however, yoga, tai chi, and chi kung involve the mind, emotions, and spirit as well as the body. Perhaps it is more accurate to describe them as ways of being, for their psychological and spiritual components are as important as their physical ones. In fact, one of the objectives of these disciplines is to promote harmony and balance between the various parts of ourselves instead of viewing mind and body as separate entities.

But you don't have to subscribe to a particular religious or cultural philosophy in order to reap health benefits. Studies repeatedly show that people who regularly engage in yoga, tai chi, and chi kung experience improvements in their circulation, respiration, blood pressure, organ functioning, flexibility, muscle tone, sleep patterns, and mental focus. Many report a heightened sense of well-being and lower levels of stress.

Another reason these Eastern-based practices are becoming so popular in the West is that anyone can do them. As Janet Green Garrison, a long-time yoga teacher in Gloucester, Massachusetts, points out, "The wonderful thing about yoga is there's a style for everybody—even if you're bedridden." Admittedly, some yoga postures require exceptional flexibility and strength, but others are easy enough for individuals with limited mobility and vitality to perform. Tai chi and chi kung involve many gentle movements that people of any age or fitness level can handle.

Yoga, tai chi, and other Eastern health practices are now common fare at YMCAs, colleges, athletic clubs, and fitness centers throughout the country. Some corporations recommend these disciplines to their employees for stress management, and professional athletes often incorporate them into their training programs.

Different Types of Chi

You don't have to become an expert in Chinese medicine to take good care of your chi. It can be helpful, though, to understand just a little about the different types of chi, where they come from, and how they function in your body. Usually, we simply use the blanket term "chi," but in actuality there are a number of variations on this basic theme.

Yuan chi or "original chi" is the primordial energy inherited from your parents.

Jen chi, also called "true energy," results from the basic body functions, including digestion, metabolism, and respiration. It is produced in the blood from nutrients in your diet.

Gu chi is derived from the food you eat.

Kong chi comes from the air you breathe and is processed by the lungs.

Zong chi results from the mixture of gu chi and kong chi.

Ying chi, also known as "nutritive chi," activates your system. It travels through the meridians to fuel the cells, organs, and metabolism. Its power depends on your intake of food, water, and air.

Zheng chi or "normal chi" is zong chi that has been activated or catalyzed by original yuan chi. This is what circulates through the body. In a sense, zheng chi results from a combination of heredity, lifestyle, and environment.

Dzang and **fu chi,** or "organ chi," flows through the various organs. As it interacts with the organs it takes on their characteristics, thus its activity in the lungs will be somewhat different than in the liver. Dzang is yin, fu is yang. Balancing these two complementary types of chi promotes good health.

Jing chi comes from the conversion of the hormones, neurochemicals, and sexual fluids. It circulates through the body's meridians to enhance immunity, promote mental clarity, and improve stamina.

Wei chi is defensive chi that circulates outside the physical body and protects it from external threats such as cold and germs.

Ling chi is spiritual energy, the purest and most subtle form of chi. This highly refined vital energy increases spiritual awareness.

Shi chi is a term for drawing external chi into the body through energy points, including those in the palms of the hands and the soles of the feet.

Shing chi describes the circulation of vital energy through the body, eliminating blockages so chi can nourish the cells, organs, and so on.

Pai chi is a method of expelling stagnant or unwanted chi from the body, through specific energy centers or via the breath.

Huan chi refers to the exchange of personal chi and external chi to replenish the body with fresh, healthy energy from a pure source.

Yang chi is a process for cultivating chi in the body.

Lien chi uses the mind and breath to refine, purify, and strengthen your vital energy.

Hua chi is a sort of internal alchemy process which transforms chi into a higher and more refined energy.

Fa chi is a technique used by master healers to transfer some of their own chi to patients (*The Complete Illustrated Guide to Chinese Medicine*, 1998).

Chi and Feng Shui

Chi also flows through our environment, activating it in much the same way as it energizes our bodies. Feng shui (pronounced *fung shway*) is the art of manipulating the movement of chi through a building or other space so that its life-giving energy encourages the health and happiness of the people who occupy the space.

Literally, feng shui means "wind" and "water." A feng shui practitioner's goal is to direct chi so that its movement resembles a gently flowing stream or a pleasant breeze. When chi gets stuck in our living and work spaces, problems can occur just as they do when chi becomes blocked in the body. Finances may languish, relationships with other people may be hampered, health may deteriorate. Chi that moves too rapidly can cause problems, too. Money may go out as quickly as it comes in, relationships may be unsettled, tension may damage health.

One of the most common impediments to chi in your home or workplace is clutter. Awkwardly placed furniture, architectural obstructions, and other obstacles can also interfere with the smooth flow of chi. Chi moves through your home in much the same way as you do. If you can walk comfortably through the different rooms of your home, it will be easy for chi to circulate smoothly and harmoniously.

Feng shui practitioners use a variety of solutions known as "cures" to fix energetic imbalances in an environment. In much the same way an acupuncturist's needles keep chi moving harmoniously through the body, feng shui cures, which include such things as light, sound, plants, mobiles, wind chimes, and mirrors, enable chi to flow properly through your home or workplace and keep it healthy. (See my books *10-Minute Feng Shui* and *10-Minute Clutter Control* for more information about feng shui.)

CHAPTER TWO

Recognizing CHI in Yourself and YOUR ENVIRONMENT

*e*ven though you can't see, hear, smell, taste, or measure chi using ordinary equipment, you can sense its presence in your body and in your environment. In fact, you probably feel chi operating in and around you every day—you just don't know how to describe what you are experiencing.

Have you ever walked into a room and picked up "bad vibes"? You may have been reacting to the presence of what's known as *sha,* a disruption in the harmonious flow of chi. Have you ever stood beside a waterfall and felt an uplifting, peaceful sensation? That's because positive chi is generated by falling water. Perhaps you've sensed another person's chi, intuitively responding to his or her sadness, joy, vitality, or fatigue, even though that person demonstrated no outward signs. Once you start paying attention to chi, you'll be able to gauge it intuitively.

Here's an exercise that helps you become aware of your own chi. Sit in a comfortable spot with your feet on the floor and your back straight. Close your eyes and take a few slow, deep breaths, until you feel relaxed and calm. Hold your hands up in front of you, chest high and about a foot apart, with your palms facing each other. Gradually move your hands closer together until your palms are only a few inches apart. Can you feel the energy flowing between them? You may sense warmth, coolness, slight pressure, or tingling. Move your hands in and out—at what point do you start to notice the presence of chi?

Now hold one hand a few inches above the opposite arm and slowly move your hand toward your shoulder. What do you experience? Next, hold one hand a few inches from your heart with the palm facing your body. Move your hand slowly down to your abdomen, then back up to your chest. Can you feel your hand "touching" your subtle body?

Now try this exercise with a friend. Sit with your eyes closed while your friend holds one palm a few inches from the back of your head. Can you detect the presence of your friend's hand? Can your friend feel your energy? Ask your friend to slide his or her hand slowly down your back, still keeping it a few inches away from your body, while you try to sense its motion. Are there places where the impression of contact is stronger than others? Then switch places and see if your friend can feel your hand brushing his or her energy field.

The practice of kinesiology helps you determine which things strengthen or weaken your chi. Here's a simple kinesiology technique you can do with a friend to test your own responses.

Lie on your back and hold a carrot in your left hand. Hold your right arm straight up, perpendicular with your body. Ask your friend to try to push your arm down while you resist. Notice how much effort it takes for your friend to move your arm. Now hold an unlit cigarette in your left hand while your friend attempts to push your arm down. Notice how much harder it is to resist the pressure your friend exerts on your arm. Your chi is weakened by the proximity of the cigarette. Experiment with various foods and substances—sugar, nuts, grains, vitamins, herbs, and so on—to see which ones nourish your chi and which ones deplete it.

Yin and Yang

Many cosmologies perceive the world as embodying two complementary forces: masculine and feminine. In the East, these fundamental energies are called *yin* (feminine) and *yang* (masculine). These primordial forces are omnipresent, everywhere, in everything. They are entwined and interdependent—neither can exist without the other.

Yin is considered to be yielding, receptive, cold, inner-directed; yang is assertive, active, hot, outer-oriented. The yin force is present in darkness, water, silence, curved shapes, cool colors. Yang abides in light, fire, noise, sharp lines, bright colors. Yin energy is restful; yang is stimulating.

Our world is a tapestry of interwoven yin and yang energies. Take a walk in a cool, wooded area or sit beside a cascading mountain stream and you'll immerse yourself in yin energy. Trek across a desert and you'll understand the yang force. The Louisiana bayou and Cape Ann, Massachusetts, are predominately yin locales. Central Texas and the Sahara are obvious yang regions.

When yin and yang are balanced, health, happiness, and well-being result. When one or the other dominates, illness and disharmony can occur. For instance, you may experience chills when there's too much yin energy in the body, whereas an excess of yang might cause you to feel feverish. Chinese medicine sees disease as a pattern of imbalance between yin and yang, and seeks to restore equilibrium by counteracting one force with the other. When you take a hot bath or drink a cup of hot tea after getting a chill, you are intuitively implementing this ancient healing philosophy.

Establishing harmony between yin and yang is also a goal of feng shui. Feng shui, as we discussed in Chapter 1, is the art of balancing chi in your living or work space. You don't have to be a feng shui master to sense the presence of yin and yang in a building—just pay attention to your immediate impressions when you enter a space. A room where the yin force is strong will seem cool, calm, perhaps private or confined. It encourages stillness and introspection. By contrast, a room with lots of yang energy in it feels warm and stimulating—a place for socializing and activity.

Feng shui practitioners employ various yin and yang cures to create balance in our environments. For example, adding plants or an aquarium could offset a preponderance of yang energy. Warm colors might be used to correct too much yin energy. (For more detailed information about feng shui cures, see my books *10-Minute Feng Shui* and *10-Minute Clutter Control.*)

Undoubtedly, you've performed simple feng shui cures to balance chi without even realizing it. When you enter a dark foyer, for instance, you feel awkward because the yin force is too powerful. Your natural reaction is to turn on a light (yang) to balance the energies.

The next time you walk into a room—especially one you've never been in before—try to sense the presence and quality of its chi. Notice your immediate impressions upon entering the room. Do you feel calm and comfortable? Or would you prefer to leave the room as quickly as possible? As you move through the room, do you detect warm or cold spots? Are there places you'd like to linger? Places where you feel blocked or unwelcome? Areas that seem heavy or murky? Others that feel irritating or unsettled?

Try to attune yourself to the subtle energies and vibrations that exist in various environments. Pay attention to your own reactions, how your personal chi is affected by ambient chi. Use your intuition. Part of the art of feng shui is the ability to sense how chi operates so you can manipulate it to create situations that nurture and support you.

Earth Chi

Many earth-honoring traditions view the earth as a living entity. If you think of the earth as a "body," chi is the breath that animates it. As chi circulates through the earth, it influences the plants, animals, people, and other life forms that inhabit our planet.

Geomancers, who sense and work with the life force in the earth, can map invisible energy lines running through the land. Dowsers, feng shui masters, and other geomancers use special tools such as rods, pendulums, and compasses to detect the patterns of earth energies. Some of these lines are constructive, others are destructive. In Britain, these energy patterns are known as ley lines (pronounced *lay*) and many ancient sacred sites, such as Stonehenge and Glastonbury, are located along the most powerful ley lines.

In China, the auspicious energy lines are said to be conduits for *sheng* chi or Dragon's Breath. *Shar* or "killing" chi flows through the pernicious lines. A home or business that's sited in the path of sheng chi will flourish, for this vital energy nourishes whatever it touches. But if you live or work near a channel through which shar chi flows, you may experience poor health, financial difficulties, family problems, and a host of other woes. A feng shui master's job is to rectify destructive forces and render them more benign so they support rather than damage life.

You don't have to be a geomancer to sense some of the most obvious chi patterns—you can see chi's influence manifested in topography. Low-lying areas, water, and cool, dark, enclosed places hold yin energy. The yang force is present in high mountains, sandy and rocky terrain, and hot, dry, open, windswept areas.

Nourishing chi operates in gently winding rivers and streams; harmful chi resides in stagnant pools. A house built on the top of a steep mountain peak, where it is subjected to strong winds, will suffer from the adverse effects of shar chi. But one situated on a protected, gentle slope will enjoy the benefits of sheng chi. Meandering country roads conduct sheng chi harmoniously through the landscape, but straight streets and superhighways allow shar chi to rush by, destroying peace and well-being.

Notice your own responses to particular locales. Many of the places we tend to "escape" to when we need some R&R are oases of positive chi. Realtors instinctively recognize the presence of earth energies and put high market values on homes located in areas where healthy chi abounds.

Unfortunately, modern Western societies haven't respected the land and the energy forces operating in it. We build without considering the effects of our structures on all life forms, including ourselves. As a result, our cities are often centers filled with killing chi. Sharp angles, towering skyscrapers, electricity lines, asphalt and concrete surfaces combine to produce stressful, unhealthy environments that disrupt our own chi and destroy the life-giving forces found in nature. As feng shui becomes more widely accepted in the West, perhaps we'll start paying more attention to the way chi operates in our environments and how it influences our health, wealth, and happiness.

Cosmic Chi

Chi flows to us from the heavens, too—not only from the sun's obvious life-giving energy, but from the moon and planets as well. We have only to observe the moon's effect on the tides to recognize the power this celestial body exerts on our earth. And anyone who has worked in a hospital or police department can attest to the full moon's impact on human behavior.

Western astrology observes how the energies of the heavenly bodies influence life on our planet. As Ralph Waldo Emerson expressed it, "Astrology is astronomy brought to Earth and applied to the affairs of man." Although most people think astrology is what they read in the daily horoscope column of the newspaper, it's actually an ancient and complex scientific art that can be used to detect disease, predict weather patterns, chart stock market fluctuations, and solve crimes, as well as to analyze personality.

Each of the planets and "lights" (as the sun and moon are sometimes called) generates a particular force that we on earth experience in discernible ways. These forces can be thought of as "cosmic chi." Because the earth and planets are constantly moving, their energy patterns keep shifting, causing circumstances in our lives and in our world to change.

Sometimes the influence of cosmic chi is harmonious, supportive, and comfortable. Other times, celestial energies produce tension, upsets, and difficulties. Cosmic chi can increase your vitality or weaken your resistance to illness. It can encourage prosperity or hinder your financial success. It can promote happy interactions with other people or disrupt relationships.

You'll experience the favorable effects of a planet if it was auspiciously positioned at the time of your birth or if it is currently in a positive place in the sky relative to the locations of the heavenly bodies at your birth. A planet's potentially harmful influence may be felt if it was adversely situated at the time of your birth or if it is presently in a place that is inharmonious with the positions the heavenly bodies occupied at the time of your birth.

When you understand the individual planetary forces and how they are operating in your life at any given time, you can use the energy in productive ways. Not everyone will be affected in the same way or at the same time by these forces. In Part Two, I provide some tips for working with celestial energies to encourage health, happiness, and success.

You'll need to consult with an astrologer to fully comprehend the cosmic patterns that are impacting you now—or that will in the future. To give you a general idea of the chi each planet projects and the areas of your life that will be most obviously affected by its energy, here are some brief explanations. (See my books *Planets in Signs* and *Magickal Astrology* for more detailed information.)

The sun beams life-giving, growth-producing chi toward earth.
 Without its warmth, life as we know it would cease. Solar energy strengthens your physical vitality, enhances your self-confidence,

and promotes positive actions and interactions. A powerful, activating yang force, the sun can boost your personal chi and help you feel more positive in every way. The sun governs the heart, the upper back, and the spinal column.

The moon is the sun's complement and embodies the yin force. Lunar energy affects our emotions, physical bodies, reproductive cycles, the subconscious, the tides, and weather patterns. You may notice that your moods and vitality change in connection with the moon's phases. The brain, breasts, uterus, sympathetic nervous system, lymphatic system, glands, and digestive organs are controlled by the moon.

Mercury plays a role in all forms of communication, conscious mental activity, and movement. Its energy directly influences your interactions with other people, travel, your ability to comprehend and convey information, and manual dexterity. Every four months for three weeks at a time, Mercury goes retrograde and appears to be moving backward in its orbit. During these periods, you may experience confusion, communication breakdowns, delays when traveling, and other mix-ups. These are good times to rest, turn inward, or take a vacation. Mercury rules the hands, arms, lungs, collarbones, optic nerve, nervous system, sense of smell, thyroid, thymus, and vocal cords.

Venus is the planet of relationships and astrologers connect it with love, pleasure, sensuality, beauty, friendship, and harmony. Its energy also supports creativity and artistic pursuits. The chi generated by Venus usually makes you feel more sociable, optimistic, and cheerful. Venus governs the kidneys, lower back, veins and blood circulation, female genitals, ovaries, and throat.

Mars is the primary yang force in the cosmos. Its energy is active and stimulating. Martian chi can enhance your vitality or create tension in your life. Often it stirs up impatience, assertiveness, and a desire for physical movement—in some cases, carelessness and impulsiveness may result in accidents or injuries. Mars influences the adrenal glands, muscles, male genitals, head, and face.

Jupiter also projects a strong yang force. Its energy is expansive and enlivening. Jupiter's chi makes you feel upbeat, adventurous, self-confident, and outgoing. Under this planet's influence your health and vitality generally improve, though you may gain weight. Jupiter rules the thighs, liver, blood, and pituitary gland.

Saturn's yin energy is contracting and solidifying. This planet's chi tends to be sluggish and heavy. Under Saturn's influence you may feel devitalized, limited, withdrawn, pessimistic, and overworked—it's a good idea to get more rest and TLC during these periods. Saturn governs the bones, teeth, skin, and knees.

Uranus is the planet of change, and it frequently generates shifts, breaks, or upsets of some kind in your life. Its dynamic yang energy produces tension, impulsiveness, and irritability that can lead to stress-related health problems or accidents. On the positive side, Uranus can stimulate intellectual breakthroughs and insights. Uranus influences the nervous system, calves, and ankles.

Neptune's "job" is to dissolve physical boundaries and structures. This planet's powerful yin force can cause you to feel devitalized, confused, and overly sensitive (physically and emotionally). Allergies and infections are common under its influence. On the positive side, Neptune tends to enhance your intuition and imagination. It rules the feet, emotions, body fluids, and pineal gland.

Pluto is associated with change, destruction, and death. Its influence usually prompts some sort of major change that involves breaking down old, worn-out structures to make room for new growth.

This planet's powerful force combines yin and yang, and its energy is highly focused, intense, and unyielding. Under its influence, you may become motivated to take charge of your life, make important changes, or feel as if you are being governed by forces beyond your control. In some cases, Pluto can play a role in cancer or other life-threatening illnesses and traumas. It rules the sex organs and elimination system.

CHAPTER THREE

Healing
YOUR
CHI

*t*he Chinese believe illness results when chi becomes unbalanced. Chi imbalances may be caused by heredity, diet, lifestyle, stress, trauma, weather conditions, and many other factors. Healers might treat imbalances with acupuncture, herbs, exercise, diet, and/or other remedies. Unlike conventional Western medicine, which tends to focus on removing symptoms or fixing a specific, localized complaint, Chinese medicine seeks to heal the whole system and to restore balance on every level. Chi imbalances fall into four basic categories, according to Chinese medical theory.

Deficient chi means the person doesn't have enough chi to facilitate optimal body functioning. Low vitality, apathy, susceptibility to colds and other common illnesses are characteristic of this condition. Elderly people often suffer from deficient chi.

Sinking chi is more advanced or severe than deficient chi. In this case, the level of chi is too low to maintain proper organ, tissue, or cell functioning. The body begins to deteriorate because there is too little chi to sustain it. Sinking chi may be found in people with cancer, serious immune system problems, and other "wasting" diseases.

Stagnant chi doesn't flow quickly enough through the body, resulting in energy blockages or sluggishness. In time, this can lead to problems in the organs or other tissues that are not being nourished properly.

Rebellious chi moves in the wrong direction, producing disharmony. In the stomach, for instance, rebellious chi can cause indigestion or vomiting.

Emotions and Chi

Chi and the emotions are intertwined and, in a sense, interdependent—your emotions affect chi and chi affects your emotions. When you feel happy, secure, calm, and hopeful, your positive emotions encourage the smooth flow of chi through your body. It works the other way, too—when your chi is healthy and strong, you tend to feel content. But sadness, anger, fear, nervousness, and other distressing emotions can throw your chi out of whack. And chi imbalances can produce unhappiness.

Emotional upsets can disturb the balance of chi in your system and lead to all sorts of physical ills. In our complex, fast-paced world, for example, stress has become a common emotional health problem with a wide range of resulting physical ailments including headaches, insomnia, digestive disorders, asthma, immune system deficiencies, high blood pressure, and coronary disease. Studies discussed in Dr. Lawrences Le Shan's, *You Can Fight for Your Life: Emotional Factors in the Causation of Cancer*, have linked cancer with emotional factors, especially the grief that follows the death of a loved one.

As discussed in Chapter 1, chi first enters the subtle bodies that surround the physical body. The subtle bodies closest to the physical one are known (in Western esoteric terms) as the "etheric" and the "emotional" bodies. Illnesses occur as disruptions in these subtle energy fields before materializing in physical form.

Chinese medicine considers seven emotions to be harmful to chi: joy, anger, sadness, grief, pensiveness, fear, and fright. To most Westerners, sadness and grief seem pretty similar, as do fear and fright, but the Chinese make distinctions based on how these emotional states affect chi and which organs they impact. We might also have trouble understanding how joy can be problematic. Because balance is one of the primary concerns of Chinese medicine, too much joy can produce an imbalance, just as too much thinking (pensiveness) can. According to Chinese medicine, chronic unresolved fear can damage the kidneys. Anger harms the liver, grief adversely impacts the lungs, and too much pensiveness can injure the spleen.

Western holistic healers agree that positive emotions support and encourage good health, whereas negative ones can lead to illness. Homeopathy, for instance, addresses emotional and psychological conditions in order to rectify physical complaints. I was once treated homeopathically for asthma and diagnosed as suffering from perfectionism. After being given a homeopathic remedy called *arum*, which is derived from gold, the asthma improved. (Someone else's asthma might be rooted in anger or another emotion, however, and be treated with a different remedy.)

Best-selling author Louise Hay is one of many to write about the body-mind link in health. Hay explains that our bodies continually "talk" to us, telling us how our emotions are influencing us physically. We even use sayings that graphically describe this connection. Is someone giving you a "pain in the neck"? Does your upper back ache from "carrying the world on your shoulders"?

Many of the tips and techniques given in Part Two recommend ways to bolster and balance your chi by lifting or moderating your emotions. A variety of holistic healing modalities are suggested, as well as numerous self-help treatments that can have a positive impact on your chi.

What Is Holistic Healing?

During the last quarter-century, holistic healing concepts and complementary therapies have begun to gain acceptance in the West. In 1992, the *Journal of the American Medical Association* reported that about one-third of all Americans use alternative medical therapies. A study done by Harvard University found that in 1997 Americans spent 72 billion on alternative treatments and made more than 600 million visits to complementary health practitioners (compared to 368 million visits to their primary care physicians)—an increase of almost 50 percent since 1990.

Generally speaking, holistic healing modalities take the entire system into consideration and treat all levels of being, not just the physical body. Some practitioners prefer the spelling "wholistic" because healing involves the whole person. Body, mind, emotions, and spirit are viewed as inseparable—all affect your health, and all must be considered in the course of treating an ailment. For example, many holistic practitioners believe that the reason cancer "comes back" after chemotherapy or surgery—sometimes in another part of the body—is because the underlying psychological problems that initially led to the formation of cancerous tumors have not been cleared up.

Holistic healing also targets the subtle bodies and the life force or chi. Some types of "vibrational medicine" such as homeopathy and flower essences don't even contain any measurable amounts of the substance used in the remedy—they work at the level of the subtle energy bodies, which in turn produces physical results. (Indeed, allopathic Western medicine argues that the doses are so small they couldn't possibly have an impact; therefore if healing occurs it must be due to the placebo effect.)

Although "new" to Westerners, many complementary healing practices have ancient roots. Acupuncture, for instance, has been performed in the East for thousands of years. Massage and aromatherapy were popular in ancient Egypt. Herbalism, which is still the primary form of medicine used in many parts of the world today, predates written records.

As is true of conventional, allopathic medical techniques, proficiency in holistic healing requires study and experience. Acupuncture and chiropractic, for example, demand extensive knowledge of anatomy and great skill. Some therapies, such as herbalism, can be dangerous if practiced incorrectly. Others, such as flower remedies and aromatherapy, can generally be used without risk, and homeopathy is rarely harmful—just ineffective if you choose the wrong remedy. To be safe, it is always a good idea to consult a competent professional rather than attempting to diagnose and treat illnesses yourself.

An Overview of Holistic Healing Modalities

Fundamentally, taking care of your chi involves caring for yourself on every level and following a lifestyle that promotes health and well-being—physically, mentally, emotionally, and spiritually. In Part Two, I offer a variety of tips for nurturing and balancing your chi that draw upon holistic healing therapies. Each of these modalities is a field in itself and scores of wonderful books have been written about them (I've listed some in the Resources section). To lay the groundwork, however, here are brief descriptions of some of the most popular complementary healing techniques to help you decide which ones you might want to investigate further.

Acupuncture, as discussed in Chapter 1, uses fine needles and sometimes heat to activate and balance chi. A practitioner inserts needles at certain points along the body's meridians to remove blockages and harmonize the flow of energy through the body. Acupuncture has been shown to be effective in alleviating a variety of ailments, both physical and emotional. It is particularly successful in reducing pain.

Acupressure activates the flow of chi by applying gentle pressure to the sensitive points along the meridians, instead of inserting needles into them. This less invasive therapy is good for people who are squeamish about needles and can be used as a self-help procedure alone or in conjunction with acupuncture. Shiatsu is a popular form of acupressure. Reflexology uses acupressure points in the hands and feet to harmonize the flow of chi and to heal energy imbalances in the body.

Aromatherapy primarily refers to healing through olfaction. Some aromatic essential oils can also be ingested or rubbed directly on the skin and absorbed, providing therapeutic benefits in much the same way as other herbal medicines do. (Some essences are skin irritants or toxic when taken internally, however, so be sure to use with care.)

When inhaled, scents affect the limbic system of the brain, the portion associated with memory, emotions, and sexuality—which is why certain smells have the ability to reawaken long-ago memories or stimulate the libido. The brain responds instantly to odors—shifts in brain wave function can be measured immediately after a person sniffs certain scents.

Because aromatic substances interact with the body both physiologically and psychologically, they have a wide variety of beneficial applications. Essential oils have been shown to be effective as antiseptics, deodorants, anti-inflammatory agents, fungicides, hypertensives, digestive aids, aphrodisiacs, and more.

Ayurveda, which means "Science of Life," dates back to 3,000 B.C.E. and is rooted in Indian and Hindu philosophy. Ayurvedic medicine involves balancing a life force called *prana,* (chi). It considers the forces of the wind, the tides and water, heat and the sun as significant factors in human health and well-being. Balancing the body, mind, and spirit and adapting to external forces are viewed as the keys to good health. Massaging the body's vital energy points, diet, yoga, meditation, and purification procedures all play roles in ayurvedic healing.

Bioenergetics evolved out of the work of the Austrian biologist and psychotherapist Wilhelm Reich in the 1930's and '40s. Reich theorized that traumas, painful emotions, and fears caused chronic tension in the muscles, which he called "armoring." This tension interferes with the movement of chi and can lead to myriad health problems. Bioenergetics combines movement, massage, breathing, and various physical exercises to break down this muscle armoring and release repressed emotions.

Chi kung (also spelled *qigong*) is an ancient Chinese system of promoting health and longevity by harnessing and balancing the vital life force (chi). Literally translated, it means "breath work" or "energy work." Chi kung combines proper diet, breathing techniques, rhythmic movement and exercise, and mental awareness to cultivate balance between the human body, cosmic forces, and nature's energies.

Chiropractic was founded in the late nineteenth century by B. J. Palmer, and is probably the most widely accepted "alternative" medical therapy used in the West. It involves manually adjusting the spine—and in some cases other parts of the skeletal system— to alleviate pain and other physical and emotional problems as well as to maintain overall good health. Chiropractic has been shown to be effective in relieving ailments ranging from headaches to arthritis—indeed, the spine's integral role in virtually all body functioning suggests that the health of the entire body depends upon the condition of the spine. When the spine is properly aligned, chi can move freely through the body.

Chromotherapy, also known as color healing, generally focuses colored light on the body to promote healing, although sometimes treatment involves looking at a particular color, visualizing it mentally, or "breathing" it. Studies have shown that being in the presence of certain colors can cause emotional and physical responses, for instance, sitting in a red room can increase respiration and body temperature whereas sitting in a blue room has the opposite effect. Colors are used to stimulate, calm, balance, and otherwise induce physical and emotional healing.

Crystal/gemstone therapy is an ancient practice that taps the energetic vibrations of particular gems and quartz crystal for therapeutic purposes. Long before gems were prized for their monetary worth, people valued them for their healing powers. Today, healers may place crystals and gemstones on specific parts of the body or in a patient's energy field to strengthen, calm, balance, cleanse, or otherwise rectify disturbances. Crystals and gemstones are also used to "charge" water, herbs, and other remedies as well as in conjunction with other forms of treatment.

Flower remedies were initially developed by the English physician Dr. Edward Bach in the 1930s. The plant's essence or chi is distilled by placing flowers in bowls of water and setting them in sunlight, which allows their life forces and healing vibrations to infuse into the water. The liquid is then diluted and potentized—no physical plant substance exists, only the life force. Each flower possesses specific characteristics that, when the liquid is ingested, interact with a person's subtle energy bodies to promote emotional, mental, and physical healing. Bleeding Heart, for instance, helps to soothe the pain of a broken heart; impatiens calms restlessness and irritability connected with impatience.

Herbalism is one of the oldest forms of medicine and it's still the most frequently used in many parts of the world. The healing properties contained in plants may be extracted and utilized in various ways—drunk in tea, applied directly to the skin in poultices or compresses, and ingested in pill form (like vitamins) or in tinctures (concentrated liquid herbal mixtures). Although many herbs, such as chamomile and lemongrass, may be taken by most people safely, others can be harmful if used incorrectly and should be administered by a trained professional.

Homeopathy was founded by the German physician Dr. Samuel Hahnemann during the late 1700s and early 1800s. Hahnemann based his theory on the law of similars or "like cures like," a concept that has been with us since the time of Hippocrates. A patient is treated with a minute amount of a substance whose effects on the human body are similar to the symptoms the patient is experiencing—or a substance that would cause such symptoms in a healthy person if administered in a full-strength dose. The objective is to enhance the body's natural ability to heal itself by stimulating the defense system. According to Nigel and Susan Garion-Hutchings, authors of *The New Concise Guide to Homeopathy,* "A symptom is the outward sign of the inner disease of the vital force, which is struggling to throw out those harmful forces or patterns of behavior which threaten to harm the whole being."

Hypnotherapy uses hypnosis to encourage emotional or physical healing. For most people, the hypnotic trance is similar to a deeply relaxed, meditative, alpha state and it can be measured clinically with an encephalograph. It becomes hypnosis when in that relaxed state you institute a thought process to effect a change. During this altered state, a post-hypnotic suggestion may be given that will remain in effect after the person comes out of the trance. Many people have experienced good results using hypnosis to overcome habits such as smoking or overeating, fears such as stage fright, and to manage pain. In these instances, the hypnotist's suggestions strengthen the patient's own resolve, rather than overriding it. The idea that a hypnotized patient is unconscious is a fallacy—most people actually experience a heightened sense of awareness while under hypnosis.

Massage has been practiced for 5,000 years and was a favorite treatment of Hippocrates. Many different types of massage are popular today for relieving discomforts ranging from childbirth to sports injuries to arthritis. So-called "Swedish" massage generally involves rubbing the muscles and stroking the skin to promote relaxation and circulation. "Shiatsu" massage incorporates acupuncture principles, applying gentle pressure instead of needles to activate the energy points along the body's meridians.

Osteopathy was devised by an American army surgeon named Andrew Taylor Still in 1874. It treats the body's structure: the skeleton, muscles, ligaments, and connective tissue. Osteopaths believe that when one part of your system is out of balance, other parts of your body as well as your mental and emotional states will be impaired. The reverse is also true: Mental and emotional disturbances reveal themselves in the body's structure, and can be remedied by manipulating the physical body. For example, stretching and loosening the muscles allows chi to flow more freely; adjusting improper posture or joints increases a patient's mobility and chi's movement as well. Cranial osteopathy gently manipulates the bones of the skull to heal problems in the head, such as sinus trouble, headaches, and tinnitus. Osteopathy can be used to treat injuries or as part of an ongoing program of well-being.

Polarity was developed by an Australian chiropractor and osteopath named Randolph Stone who studied Asian medicine and spirituality. This form of bodywork involves balancing the flow of energy through the *chakras* (see pages 61–63). According to Polarity theory, the life force (chi) circulates through the body in a double helix pattern, crossing at each of the chakras. Polarity therapy may include cleansing, diet, exercise, and counseling as well as touch to promote overall wellness.

Reflexology involves massaging the feet and hands to stimulate and balance the flow of chi. According to this form of massage therapy, which dates back to ancient Egypt and Greece, each part of the body corresponds to a spot on your feet and hands. By rubbing and pressing these points, you activate the flow of chi to the related organs, tissues, or cells. For instance, the toes are linked with the head—the eyes, ears, sinuses, teeth, brain, and so on. The heel contains points that connect with the pelvis and sciatic nerve.

Reiki actually means Universal Life Force Energy (or chi), although the term is used interchangeably with the practice of focusing chi for emotional and physical healing. More accurately, the techniques involved are called the Usui System of Natural Healing, after the founder Dr. Mikao Usui. A Reiki healer places his or her hands on a patient and, by focusing intention, channels chi and directs it to flow into the patient in a way that is balancing and enlivening.

Sound healing proposes that each note of the musical scale corresponds in vibration to a particular part of the body. Sound waves are directed to the area where healing is needed in order to restore proper functioning. Chanting or intoning certain notes or chords is an ancient form of sound healing, practiced by the Druids as well as the Tibetan monks. Musical instruments can also be played to encourage healing. Drumming can break up energetic blockages in the body and allow chi to flow more smoothly. Crystal or metal "singing" bowls, tuned to specific frequencies, are often used to harmonize the chakras and send healing vibrations to the body's organs, tissues, and so on.

Visualization has been popularized by writer Shakti Gawain and others as a way to heal physical and emotional problems. Usually combined with meditation, it involves creating a mental image of a condition you desire in order to facilitate mind-body healing. Visualization's operating principle suggests that before something can manifest in the physical world it must exist in the mind. When you imagine yourself well, your mind directs the body to carry out your objective.

Yoga is thousands of years old—no one really knows how long it has been practiced in the East—although it didn't gain a strong following in the West until the 1960s. Yoga combines physical movement with mental relaxation and deep, rhythmic breathing to produce overall health. The most popular form of yoga in the U.S. is "Hatha," which involves holding various postures or *asanas* to strengthen the body, increase balance, and improve flexibility. However, there are many different types of yoga, both gentle and strenuous, that can be performed by people of all ages and physical conditions. Athletes, pregnant women, people recovering from injuries, the elderly, even toddlers can benefit from yoga.

The Chakras

Healing and balancing the *chakras* is an objective of many holistic healing therapies. Chakra is a Sanskrit term meaning wheel. To psychics and others who can see them, these nonphysical energy centers resemble spinning wheels located roughly along the spine. Even if you can't see them, you may be able to sense their presence in your own body. For instance, if you were to play a singing bowl that's attuned to a particular chakra, you might feel a slight tingling, warmth, or rush of energy in the corresponding chakra.

The life force travels up the spinal column and energizes these vortices. When the chakras become blocked or don't operate properly, illness occurs. Health and happiness result when the life force flows freely and harmoniously through the chakras. Some of the tips in Part Two are designed to help you balance these energy centers.

Emotions and attitudes affect the chakras, as well as the subtle bodies and chi. If we look at both the emotional and the physical areas associated with a particular chakra, we may be able to discover an ailment's cause and its cure. For instance, the sacral chakra is located in the region of the lower back and governs sexuality. It's no surprise, then, that couples who are experiencing relationship troubles often suffer from lower back pain.

In her book *Awakening Intuition,* Dr. Mona Lisa Schulz notes that "when someone with lower back pain and marital problems undertakes marriage counseling with his or her partner, the lower back pain often improves significantly, without benefit of surgery or medication, as the relationship improves."

Each chakra corresponds to a color of the visible spectrum and a note of the musical scale, consequently, chromotherapy and sound healing can be particularly effective in chakra work. Astrologers also link the chakras with the planets. Eastern healing and spiritual traditions consider these seven main chakras to be most important.

Root chakra—located at the base of the spine, this energy center is associated with the survival instinct and your sense of security. It controls the bones, teeth, spine, rectum, and colon. The root chakra's color is red and its musical note is C.

Sacral chakra—found near the abdomen in the vicinity of the lower back, about a hand's width below the belly button, this chakra is related to creativity and sexuality. The reproductive organs, kidneys, and bladder are influenced by the sacral chakra. Its color is orange and its musical note is D.

Solar plexus chakra—located at the solar plexus, about halfway between your belly button and heart, this chakra is connected with the will and personal power. It controls the stomach, liver, digestive system, spleen, gall bladder, the autonomic nervous system, and the muscles. Its color is yellow and its musical note is E.

Heart chakra—situated near the heart, this chakra regulates the heart, blood circulation, skin, chest, and upper back. The center of love and emotions, its color is green and its musical note is F.

Throat chakra—found at the base of the neck, between the collarbones, this chakra is associated with self-expression and communication. The jaw, neck, voice, upper lungs, and arms are controlled by the throat chakra. Its color is blue and its musical note is G.

Brow chakra—located on the forehead between the eyebrows, at the site of the "third eye," this chakra is the center of intuition. It controls the endocrine system, nose, left brain, and left eye. Its color is indigo and its musical note is A.

Crown chakra—situated at the top of the head, the crown chakra is associated with the soul and your connection to the Divine. The nervous system, cerebrum, right brain, and right eye are controlled by this chakra. Its color is violet and its musical note is B.

PART
TWO

CHAPTER FOUR

The Care and Feeding of YOUR BODY

*a*lthough well-being requires an integration of mind-body-spirit, and complementary therapies actually work on many levels, this chapter focuses on tips and techniques that primarily involve physical practices to promote healthy chi.

Breathe deeply and rhythmically.

The air we breathe is a main source of chi. One of the simplest ways to facilitate the healthy movement of chi through your body is to breathe deeply, fully, and rhythmically. Most of us, however, inhale shallowly and don't exhale completely. When we are upset or under stress, we may hold our breath or take many short, irregular breaths. Become conscious of the way you breathe and, if necessary, adjust your breathing patterns. When you inhale, fill your lungs and allow your chest and abdomen to expand. When you exhale, dispel as much air as possible from your lungs. Proper breathing increases the amount of oxygen in your bloodstream and improves circulation. Slow, deep, rhythmic breathing also relieves tension and can help you stay calm under pressure.

Don't smoke.

By now, nearly everyone is aware of the dangers associated with cigarette smoking. Hundreds of thousands of people die each year from smoking-related causes. Even occasional smoking taints the chi in the air your breathe and brings toxins into your lungs. Over time, it can damage tissues, interfere with proper breathing and chi circulation, and contribute to numerous other serious health conditions.

Practice yogic breathing, technique #1.

Breathing is an integral part of yoga. One simple technique involves breathing through one nostril first, then the other. Press your finger to the left side of your nose to close off the left nostril while you inhale through your right nostril. Then, release your left nostril and exhale through it. Next, alternate the process, closing off your right nostril while you inhale through your left nostril. Release your right nostril and exhale through it. Repeat this cycle several times.

Yogic breathing, technique #2.

Sit quietly with your back straight and your feet flat on the floor. Close your eyes and inhale slowly to a count of four. Hold your breath for a count of four. Then exhale slowly to a count of four. Repeat this breathing pattern three times. This technique helps to regulate and balance the flow of chi—it's also a quick, safe, and easy cure for hiccups.

Stand up and stretch at least once per hour.

This exercise is especially important if you spend a lot of time sitting at a desk or in front of a computer. Get up at least once each hour and stretch your arms up over your head, then out to your sides. Twist at the waist, bend over and try to touch your toes, shrug your shoulders, turn your neck from side to side, do a few knee bends, wriggle your fingers—whatever movements help you to loosen up those stiff joints and muscles. (If necessary, set a timer to remind you to get up and move your body.)

Sit up straight.

Pay attention to your posture when seated. People who spend long periods of time at a desk or in front of a computer are particularly susceptible to poor posture that can block chi. When you slouch or slump in your seat, your spine bends in an unnatural way. Your stomach, chest, and other parts of the body become compressed, making it difficult for chi to move freely. When you sit up straight, with your back and torso properly aligned, chi can flow through your body with ease.

Keep your spine straight when you stand.

Did you ever try to walk while balancing a book on your head? It's good practice for maintaining good posture. The spine is one of the most important conduits for chi, but improper posture can interfere with chi's movement. Hold your head high and keep your spine straight when you stand to facilitate the flow of chi into all parts of your body.

Bend your knees slightly while standing.

If you lock your knees while standing, you can interfere with the smooth flow of chi between the lower and upper parts of your body. This rigid stance also puts more pressure on your back. Instead, keep you knees slightly bent, which relieves tension on your back and strengthens your leg muscles.

Exercise your neck muscles.

Your head weighs about as much as a bowling ball, so it's no wonder your neck may get stiff from the effort of holding it up. This is especially likely if you tend to spend a lot of time bent over a desk, staring at a computer screen, driving, or doing repetitive tasks that put strain on your neck. Periodically throughout the day, exercise your neck muscles by turning your head slowly from side to side ten times. Next, tilt your head forward and backward ten times, gently stretching your neck muscles. Finally, lean your head slowly toward your right shoulder ten times, then toward your left shoulder. This exercise relieves tension in your neck and shoulders, and lets chi flow more smoothly between your head and body.

Shrug your shoulders.

One of the places tension is most likely to develop is in the shoulders. This prevents chi from flowing easily between your head and your body. Several times a day, shrug your shoulders to loosen tight muscles. Raise and lower both shoulders at the same time, repeating this motion eight times. Then, raise and lower each shoulder individually. Move your shoulders back and forth as well as up and down, in a circling motion. Roll each shoulder in this manner eight times.

Coordinate bending and breathing.

Stand with your feet slightly apart and stretch your arms up over your head as high as you comfortably can. As you raise your arms, inhale slowly until your lungs are full. Then bend forward at the waist, keeping your knees slightly bent, while you swing your arms down and back behind you. As you bend forward, exhale quickly, emptying all the air from your lungs. Return to a standing position, and inhale deeply as you stretch your arms back up over your head again. Repeat this exercise several times to stimulate the flow of chi. This procedure also helps loosen tight shoulder, back, neck, and arm muscles.

Relax your jaw.

Do you tend to clench your teeth when you are under stress? The next time you're driving in heavy traffic or rushing to meet a deadline, notice the tension in your jaw. Open and close your mouth a few times to loosen the tightness. You may want to keep your mouth slightly open during stressful times to reduce tension in your jaw.

Get regular chiropractic adjustments.

Most of us only go to a chiropractor if we injure ourselves. But pain is just one manifestation of improper skeletal alignment. When your spine is out of alignment, energy becomes blocked—and because the spine is so important to total health, stagnant chi in your back can lead to myriad health problems. Regular chiropractic adjustments keep your skeletal system properly aligned, enabling chi to flow freely through your spine to nourish your entire body.

Visit an osteopath.

Like chiropractic, osteopathic adjustments can be part of an overall health maintenance program as well as a treatment for pain or specific physical problems. When the body's structure (bones, muscles, and connective tissue) are correctly aligned, chi can flow smoothly, blood circulates properly, and the body can heal itself.

Treat yourself to regular massages.

Stress, lack of exercise, overwork, extensive computer use, and emotional problems can lead to tight muscles. When muscles remain in a constant state of tension, without compensating relaxation, they can actually pull bones out of alignment and interfere with healthy functioning of the digestive, respiratory, and circulation systems. All this blocks the smooth flow of chi to various parts of the body. Full body massage is one of the best ways to relieve muscle tension and restore healthy movement in all parts of your body. It also feels great!

Massage your feet.

According to reflexology, or foot massage therapy, each part
of the body corresponds to a spot on the soles of your feet. For
instance, the toes are linked with the head—the eyes, ears, sinuses,
teeth, brain, and so on. The heel contains points that connect with the
pelvis and sciatic nerve. By massaging the feet, you can stimulate the
flow of chi throughout your entire body. Gently press and rub the soles
of your feet, paying special attention to the areas that are painful or
seem tight. These sore spots relate to parts of your body where energy is
blocked. Take a few minutes each day to massage these spots. Gradually,
you'll reduce body tension and improve the movement of chi through
your system.

Massage your hands.

Your hands, too, contain pressure points that correspond to other parts of the body. The fingers, for instance, relate to the different parts of the head, the center of the palm to the internal organs. You can increase the flow of chi to various areas of your body by massaging your hands. Gently pull each finger and thumb, then wriggle all your fingers. Rub the palms and backs of your hands. Ball your fingers into fists, then stretch them open as wide as you can. Pay special attention to any spots that are tender or tight—these relate to parts of your body where energy is blocked and may need a little TLC. Massaging your hands several times a day can help to keep chi flowing smoothly to all parts of your body.

Wear comfortable shoes.

Your feet endure a great deal of punishment every day simply supporting the weight of your body. High heels, pointed toes, or shoes that don't fit properly do more than just injure your feet; they can throw your whole body out of alignment. Wear comfortable shoes that provide correct support for your feet and body. If necessary, have orthopedic inserts made for your shoes to adjust your posture and balance.

Get an acupuncture treatment.

When acupuncture needles are inserted into special points or vortices along the body's meridian system, they open up energetic blockages and allow chi to move harmoniously. Chi flows into the body through these entry points and circulates to the organs via the meridian channels. (See Chapter 1 for more information.) Acupuncture can be useful in treating specific problems related to chi imbalances or as an ongoing form of therapy to support healthy chi.

Get *an acupressure treatment.*

If you're squeamish about needles, you may want to try a less invasive technique called acupressure. Rather than inserting needles, a therapist applies pressure to sensitive points in your body to balance and activate the flow of chi and remove energy blockages.

Exercise *daily.*

Our bodies weren't meant to remain stationary or to perform the same repetitive motions all day long—our ancestors used their bodies in many, diverse ways in the course of their daily tasks. To keep your chi healthy, get some sort of physical exercise daily, even if it's only for ten minutes or so. Try to combine a variety of exercises: some that involve limbering and stretching; some that are aerobic; and some that increase strength, such as weight training. Do something you enjoy—it's easier to stick with an exercise program if you like what you're doing.

Go for a walk.

Walking has a beneficial effect on chi for many reasons. It provides exercise that's not too stressful, allows you to get fresh air and sunlight, and gives you a break from your daily routine. Walking can also be a form of meditation, which helps to quiet the mind. Strolling through the woods, a park, along the beach, or other natural setting also enables you to connect with the earth and the chi that flows through the land.

Swim.

Swimming is one of the best all-around exercises for many people. In addition to improving muscle tone, circulation, respiration, and flexibility, swimming serves as a metaphor for life: If you relax, the water will buoy you; if you struggle, you'll exhaust yourself and go under.

Ride a bike.

Remember how much fun it was to ride your bike when you were a kid? It still is. Biking promotes health and well-being in numerous ways—it provides both aerobic and strengthening exercise, while exposing you to fresh air and sunshine. It's low-impact, so it puts less strain on your legs and back than running or aerobics, and it's less demanding than sports like tennis, racquetball, football, or basketball, so people of all ages can enjoy biking.

Practice yoga.

Yoga started gaining popularity in the West in the 1960s, but it has been practiced in the East for almost 5,000 years. This wonderful body-mind exercise is so diverse that almost everyone can do some form of it. Doing yoga regularly is one of the best ways to keep your chi healthy and balanced. Read a good book or watch a video to learn some of the basic postures. Or, take a yoga class at your local YMCA, fitness center, or athletic club.

Stretch like a cat.

The "cat stretch" is an easy yoga posture that helps loosen tight muscles in your back, shoulders, and neck. Kneel on all fours, then tuck your chin toward your chest and curl your back up toward the ceiling. Hold this position for a few moments, then slowly return to a flat back posture. Exhale as you curl your back, inhale as you flatten it. Repeat these movements several times. As you stretch your body, you open up the passages through your body that may have become cramped by sitting at a computer or desk all day and allow chi to flow more freely.

Rock your spine.

This yoga *asana* helps to relieve tension in your back and stimulates the flow of chi through your body. Lie on your back, preferably on a mat or carpet, and draw your knees up to your chest. Wrap your arms around your legs to support them. Gently and slowly rock back and forth. The pressure exerted on your spine helps to open up blockages and encourage the movement of chi.

Roll your spine.

This yoga exercise massages your spine and stimulates the flow of chi through your body. Lie on your back, preferably on a mat or carpet, with your knees bent and your feet close to your buttocks. Starting with your pelvis, slowly roll up your spine, trying to feel each of the vertebrae as you lift your body off the floor. Inhale as you continue rolling up until your weight is on your shoulders and your body forms an angled bridge. Then, exhale as you slowly roll your body down again from the shoulders, one vertebra at a time, until you are lying flat on your back again. Repeat this exercise three times.

Activate chi in your legs, exercise #1.

       This exercise is good for people who have cold extremities and poor circulation, because it stimulates the movement of chi into your legs and feet. Lie on your back, preferably on a mat or carpet, and extend your legs toward the ceiling, with your knees comfortably bent. Make circles in the air with your feet for about thirty seconds, first turning them one way, then the opposite way. Next, shake your legs loosely, up and down, for about thirty seconds. Then, close and open your toes ten times. Lower your legs to the floor and take a few slow, deep breaths. Repeat this series of exercises three times.

Activate chi in your legs, exercise #2.

Like the previous exercise, this one stimulates the flow of chi through the lower part of your body. Stand straight with your arms at your sides. Bend your right knee, and lift your knee up toward your chest as high as you can without straining. Return to a standing position, then bend your left knee, and lift your knee toward your chest as high as you can without straining. Repeat this series of knee lifts twenty-one times (or as often as is comfortable for you).

Stamp your feet.

This exercise activates the acupressure points in your feet and stimulates the movement of chi throughout your body. Remove your shoes and stamp your feet on the floor twenty times. You don't have to stamp hard, just enough to "wake up" the soles of your feet.

Exercise your abdominal muscles.

This easy exercise strengthens the muscles in your back and stomach, while facilitating healthy breathing. Lie on your back with your knees bent and your feet flat on the floor. Keep your arms on the floor at your sides, palms flat on the floor. Inhale slowly, filling your chest and abdomen fully with air, then gently arch your back. Exhale slowly as you lower your back and press it flat against the floor. Repeat these steps ten times.

Stretch up against a wall.

This posture opens up your chest and allows more air to flow through your lungs so you can breathe fully. It also loosens tight shoulder and arm muscles. Stand facing the wall, with your forehead leaning against it, and reach your arms up over your head. Place your palms flat against the wall. Stretch your arms and body up as far as you comfortably can. Breathe deeply to a count of four.

Perform the "sun salutation" each morning.

Performing this series of yoga postures is a great way to start the day. Face the east as you move through the various *asanas*. The movements help to balance chi and regulate the flow of energy through your body. They also exercise your muscles and improve flexibility, circulation, respiration, balance, and strength. Refer to a basic book on yoga if you aren't familiar with this series of postures.

Sway like a tree in the wind.

This exercise is good for loosening tight muscles in the upper portion of your body so chi can move freely. It also helps you connect with your center of balance. Stand with your feet about two feet apart and hold your arms out at your sides, shoulder high. Slowly lean to your left, then to your right, letting your body stretch and sway back and forth in a gentle, rhythmic motion. Don't twist your body or move your feet, though. Pay attention to your center of gravity as your upper body shifts direction. Imagine you are a graceful tree, moving your branches as the wind blows you from side to side, yet your trunk and roots remain firmly planted in the earth. If you wish, play music while you perform this exercise.

Sway like a bush in the wind.

In this variation of the previous exercise, sit on the floor with your legs crossed and your back straight. Hold your arms out at your sides, shoulder high. Slowly lean to your left, then to your right, letting your body stretch and sway back and forth in a gentle, rhythmic motion. Pay attention to your center of gravity as your upper body shifts direction. Imagine you are a bush and the wind is blowing you first one way, then the other. Feel your muscles growing looser and more flexible, allowing chi to flow freely through your body. If you wish, play music while you perform this exercise.

Pretend to fly.

Stand with your feet together and hold your arms down at your sides. Slowly raise your arms as you inhale, keeping your elbows slightly bent and your wrists relaxed. Rather than straight, your arms should be held in a graceful, rounded position. Lift your arms only as high as your shoulders, then slowly lower them, leading with your elbows, as you exhale. Let your arms come all the way down against your sides. Repeat this exercise a dozen or more times. As you move your arms, try to feel the wind under them, lifting you up, as if you were a bird flying through the sky. This exercise loosens your arms and shoulders, and facilitates healthy breathing.

Do tai chi.

Like yoga, tai chi incorporates movement, breathing, and mental focus to promote healthy chi and general well-being. Many of the gentle movements are easy enough for people of all ages and fitness levels to perform. Many YMCAs, schools, and health centers offer tai chi classes. If you can't locate a class in your area, read a book or watch a video to learn the basics.

Do chi kung.

Also spelled *qigong,* this traditional therapeutic practice is performed by thousands of Chinese each morning, in order to harmonize their chi. In major cities, groups of people can be seen doing their chi kung exercises together in parks and other public places. Read a good book on the subject or watch a video to learn some of the fundamental movements.

Catch chi in your hands, exercise #1.

According to chi kung, the hands—known as the "flags of energy"—are especially sensitive to chi. Sit quietly and comfortably, in a chair or cross-legged on the floor. Rest the backs of your hands on your thighs with your palms up. Let your fingers curl slightly. Keep your elbows bent and relaxed, your upper arms perpendicular to the floor. In this position, your hands can receive the inflow of external chi.

Catch chi in your hands, exercise #2.

Lie flat on your back with your legs spread slightly and your arms open, straight out at your sides at shoulder height. Open your hands, keeping your fingers slightly curled and your palms facing up. In this position, your hands can receive the inflow of external chi.

Circulate chi through your body.

To circulate your body's chi, sit comfortably with your hands resting on your thighs. Cup both hands, with your palms facing upward. Entwine your fingers and thumbs. This hand position encourages the circulation of internal chi through your body.

Touch your toes.

This simple exercise encourages the movement of chi through all parts of your body. Stand with your feet spread about the width of your shoulders. Hold your arms straight out at your sides, shoulder high. Bend and try to touch the fingertips of your right hand to your left toes, keeping your legs straight. Exhale as you bend. Then, straighten up and inhale. Next, bend and try to touch the fingertips of your left hand to your right toes, while you exhale. Stand up straight and inhale. If you can't reach your toes, just bend down as far as you can without straining. Perform at least ten repetitions each morning.

Dance.

Almost any type of dancing has a positive effect on chi, but dances that emphasize loose, fluid movements such as belly dancing or the whirling motions of Sufi dancing are among the best. Like all forms of exercise, dancing improves circulation, respiration, heart rate, balance, and muscle flexibility—all of which work to keep chi flowing through your body. Best of all, dancing is fun and pleasurable activities tend to have a beneficial impact on body, mind, and spirit.

Wear loose-fitting clothing.

In the Victorian era, tight corsets were fashionable and women who wore them sometimes fainted as a result of oxygen deprivation. Constricting clothing can interfere with proper breathing and the flow of chi through your body. Wear loose, comfortable clothes that don't inhibit your movement or chi.

Get more rest during the new moon.

The three days leading up to and including the new moon are generally periods of low cosmic energy. During this phase, you might feel less vital or grow tired more easily. Get more rest and try not to push yourself too hard at this time—you could tax your strength or lower your resistance to illness. Focus on rejuvenating your chi rather than allowing it to become depleted.

Get more exercise during the full moon.

Cosmic energy is highest each month during the full moon and for a day or so on either side of it. As a result, many people experience restlessness, sleeplessness, or tension in connection with this lunar phase. To help alleviate some of this excess cosmic energy, get more exercise and/or practice relaxation techniques.

Inhale eucalyptus essential oil to promote healthy breathing.

Inhaling essential oil of eucalyptus quickly opens up the nose, sinuses, and lungs so you can breathe more easily and get more beneficial chi from the air. The cool, refreshing, stimulating scent of eucalyptus can also aid colds, allergies, headaches, and minor sinus problems. To break up congestion in the lungs, rub eucalyptus-scented salve on the chest. (Note: Don't ingest!)

Take valerian to relax.

Valerian root is a gentle, non-narcotic sedative that can aid restful sleep, soothe anxiety, and promote general relaxation. Its calming properties are useful in reducing stress and balancing chi.

Take kelp to regulate metabolism.

Kelp contains a large number of vitamins and minerals that can support chi, regulate the metabolism, and help the body burn excess calories. It also sustains the nervous system and aids brain functioning.

Take goldenseal to improve respiration.

Goldenseal heals mucous membranes and aids problems in the nose, throat, and bronchial tubes to promote healthy respiration. Its natural antibiotic ability helps prevent infection and supports liver functioning. Because one of the main sources of chi is the air we breathe, goldenseal's activity can benefit the entire system.

Take evening primrose to improve digestion.

The oil of the evening primrose aids liver and spleen functioning and facilitates digestion. It can also reduce the toxic effects of a poor diet and slow the production of cholesterol. Because the food we eat is a major source of chi, evening primrose can improve the quality and amount of chi you receive.

Smile.

Smiling requires fewer muscles and less effort than frowning— it feels better, too. Practice smiling when you are alone to see how this gesture affects the way you feel. Smile at other people, even total strangers—notice how this simple act generates positive energy and good cheer.

Laugh.

Laughter is good medicine. Some studies have shown that laughter can even heal illnesses. Laughing helps to break up emotional and energetic blockages in the body, so chi can move freely. It also improves respiration and helps you breathe more deeply.

Clean up your diet.

One of the ways we take chi into our bodies is in our food. A well-balanced diet of nutritious foods leads to well-balanced and nourishing chi. Try to eliminate things from your diet that don't generate healthy chi and replace them with foods that promote beneficial chi.

Eat nuts.

Half a century ago, Edgar Cayce recommended eating almonds to prevent cancer. More recently, studies have shown that eating nuts five times per week can dramatically lower your chance of heart attack or stroke. Almonds and walnuts, in particular, contain significant amounts of vitamin E and arginine, which helps prevent blood clots. They also have a beneficial effect on cholesterol levels and improve circulation.

Eat kale.

Sulfuraphane, one of the phytochemicals in this leafy green vegetable, is a powerful anti-cancer agent. Kale is also remarkably high in vitamin E—a five ounce serving contains the equivalent of 1,200 IUs. Kale is also rich in lutein and zeanxanthine, which help prevent macular degeneration.

Eat *reishi mushrooms.*

For 4,000 years the Chinese have used mushrooms for therapeutic reasons. Reishi mushrooms, in particular, are considered to be a tonic for chi. According to Chinese medicine, they build energy, improve resistance to disease, and replenish chi that has been weakened by stress. More recently, studies in Japan have shown that reishi mushrooms can protect the liver from damage from toxic chemicals, regulate the immune system, and aid allergy sufferers.

Eat dark chocolate.

Dark chocolate contains plant substances known as polyphenols and flavonoids, which can be effective in lowering blood pressure and inhibiting blood clots that could cause stroke or heart attack. (Milk and white chocolate, however, don't offer the same benefits.) Chocolate also contains substances that stimulate the production of serotonin, the "feel-good" chemical, in the brain to produce mild feelings of euphoria similar to being in love.

Use stimulating scents to increase vitality.

Fragrances such as cinnamon, cedar, clove, and other spicy aromas have an energizing effect on the brain and can boost vitality. Put a few drops of essential oil on a handkerchief or your wrists and inhale the aroma frequently to increase vitality. If you prefer, burn a candle or incense that's scented with one of these aromas to activate chi and spice up your life.

Inhale the scent of green apple to lose weight.

Aromatherapy studies show that the crisp scent of green apple tends to suppress appetite and can be a safe, pleasant aid to dieting. Inhaling this scent can also help you relax and relieve tension headaches.

Drink a glass of red wine with dinner.

Red wine's antioxidant properties help cleanse your body of free radicals that can damage cells. (White wine doesn't offer the same benefits, however.) A glass consumed with dinner can also improve digestion, enabling you to absorb more chi from the food you eat. Some studies also show that people who drink a glass of wine per day live longer than those who completely abstain from alcoholic beverages.

Ring a gong before eating.

In China, gongs are sometimes rung before meals to disperse unwanted energies that might be present in the diners' environment. The sound of the gong balances ambient vibrations so you can eat in peace and harmony. After a while, this practice will produce an effect similar to the response in Pavlov's dogs—the sound will stimulate your digestive process and help you derive more chi from your food.

Don't eat when you are upset.

When you are tense, angry, rushed, or unhappy, your body can't digest your food properly. To glean the most nourishment from your food—and to extract healthy chi from it—eat when you are calm. Eat slowly and pay full attention to your food. Many of us watch TV or read the newspaper while eating, but these media often contain upsetting or stressful images that can interfere with good digestion. The Dalai Lama even recommends against talking while eating.

Drink green tea.

In China, green tea is a popular and healthful drink, and it's often served in Chinese restaurants in the West. Green tea's antioxidant properties help to support the body's immune system and cleanse impurities from your system. Hot tea also serves as a good antidote to cold or damp conditions that can upset the balance of chi.

Drink chamomile tea.

Tension can lead to chi imbalances. Chamomile tea is prized for its calming properties and its ability to relieve digestive upsets caused by nervousness or stress. Take a break and enjoy a hot cup of delicate chamomile tea when you feel pressured, or just before bedtime to help you sleep better. Drinking chamomile tea before a meal can also aid digestion and enable you to derive more chi from your food.

Drink ginseng tea.

This popular Asian herb is prized for its balancing properties and its ability to enhance well-being in a variety of ways. Although it is mildly energizing, it can also help relieve stress. Drinking ginseng tea can also improve concentration and aid mild depression.

Season your food with garlic.

Highly regarded as a blood purifier and general cleansing herb, garlic is an antioxidant that boosts the body's immune system. A yang herb, its warming properties can provide protection from colds and flus, and help counteract the presence of too much yin energy.

Season your food with ginger.

Ginger is a popular ingredient in many Chinese recipes, probably because it supports good digestion and helps you derive more chi from your food. Like garlic, ginger is a yang herb—whether eaten in food or drunk in tea, its warming, stimulating properties can be beneficial to colds and flus.

Play a hand drum.

Drumming stimulates the movement of chi in several beneficial ways. The rhythmic physical motion loosens the muscles in your upper body, improves circulation, and increases respiration. Contact with the drumhead activates the acupressure points in your hands to help remove energy blockages in various parts of the body. The sound breaks down obstacles in your mental and emotional space. But the best thing about drumming is that it's fun—and any enjoyable activity is advantageous to the healthy flow of chi.

Play a singing bowl.

Singing bowls are often played during meditation and rituals to attune your mind and to signal different steps in a ritual. Practitioners of sound and vibrational healing also use them to cleanse, harmonize, and heal disturbances in the human energy field and to balance the chakras. Usually made of metal alloys or crystal, these bowls emit sound waves when "played" with a leather mallet—much like running your finger around the rim of a crystal goblet. The vibration breaks up blockages in chi to restore healthy cellular patterning, and promote well-being on all levels.

Ring a bell.

In China, the pleasing sound of a bell is believed to encourage healing and balance—especially if it is tuned to one of the five sounds of the Chinese musical scale. Bells are sometimes rung during meditation and rituals to mark various steps or stages in the process, as well as to focus the meditator's mind. The ringing sound also helps disperse unwanted energies from the environment and balance ambient chi.

Go to the beach.

All four of the Western elements—earth, air, fire, and water—are present at the beach, which is one reason so many people feel drawn to seaside resorts. Immersing yourself in an environment where this ideal blend of the four elements exists has a balancing effect on your personal chi.

Chant.

Chanting plays a role in Buddhist practice as well as in many other spiritual traditions. Chanting involves the repetition of a particular sound, word, or phrase to produce a desired effect. The process works on several levels simultaneously. The physical vibration helps to stimulate, harmonize, or calm chi in the body. The rhythmic sound breaks up blockages in your energy field and in the environment. Repeating meaningful words also imprints your intention on your subconscious to encourage certain outcomes. Try chanting for several minutes a day, preferably at the same time each day, and pay attention to your experiences—while you are chanting as well as in the days and weeks that follow.

Sing.

Singing, like chanting, helps to stimulate, harmonize, or calm chi in the body. The melodic sound breaks up blockages in your energy field and in the environment, while the regulated breathing pattern circulates chi through your body. Singing offers an additional benefit, too—it's fun. Singing can also be a form of creative expression and a way to communicate with others. Lift up your voice and let yourself be heard.

Use a hula hoop.

Remember hula hoops? These kids' toys are great devices for exercising your midsection and hips. Spinning a hula hoop around your torso isn't just great for tightening your abs, though, it also activates chi at your core, in the area known as the "sea of energy," and stimulates the flow of energy through your body.

Get enough sleep.

Our bodies restore and rejuvenate themselves while we sleep. Adequate rest is essential to good health and to chi's well-being.

Pay attention to your personal diurnal cycle.

It may not be enough to simply get eight hours of sleep—the period during which you sleep can be an important factor, too. Some of us are morning people, others are night people. You may feel more rested and energetic if you go to bed at 1 A.M. and get up at 9 A.M. than if you sleep from 10 P.M. to 6 A.M. Pay attention to your personal cycle.

Take five.

Several times each day, take five-minute relaxation breaks. Close your eyes, breathe slowly and deeply, and put your cares on hold momentarily. Get away from your desk or work area. Lie down if possible. These brief respites can help keep tension from building up and refresh your mind, body, and spirit.

Pay attention to your body language.

The ways you stand, sit, walk, and use your body reveal a great deal about your feelings and attitudes. The ways you move and hold yourself also influence the movement of chi through your body. Notice your postures in different circumstances. Do you cross your arms over your chest to symbolically protect yourself when you feel defensive? Do you shake hands firmly and warmly, indicating enthusiasm and receptivity to the other person? Pay attention to the link between your body and your feelings, and to what your body language says about you.

Change the way you move.

Most of the time, we don't think much about the way we walk, stand, or sit. To become more aware of your body—and how chi moves through it—deliberately change your usual patterns of movement. If you ordinarily sit with you legs crossed at the knee, try crossing your ankles instead. If you generally open doors with your right hand, try using your left hand instead. Notice any thoughts, feelings, or sensations that arise in connection with these changes. Can you sense any shifts in your energy field? By altering habitual patterns—even simple ones—you open yourself to new possibilities and demonstrate a willingness to change old ways of doing things.

Burn candles with lead-free wicks.

Many commercially available candles use metallic wicks that contain lead. When they burn, these wicks emit toxins into the air. Because the air you breathe is one of the main sources of chi, it's best to reduce air pollution in your environment as much as possible.

Avoid cold drafts.

Chinese medicine considers both wind and cold to be harmful influences. Long-term exposure to these weather conditions not only may cause obvious, common maladies such as colds and flus, but also lead to chronic chi depletion and a deficiency of yang energy. (See Chapter 3 for more about yin and yang.)

Take a hot bath before bed.

English dramatist Dodie Smith quipped, "Noble deeds and hot baths are the best cures for depression." Depression is often linked with inadequate or unbalanced chi in the body. Therefore, activities that stimulate the flow of chi and help to remove energetic blockages caused by stress and other environmental factors can be antidotes to mild or temporary depression. Because cold causes contraction that can lead to stagnant chi, a hot soak in the tub, which relaxes tense muscles, helps chi move freely again. A hot bath—preferably one to which therapeutic essential oils have been added (see Chapter 3)—is an easy, healthful, and pleasurable way to nourish your chi.

Enjoy a foot bath.

Soaking your feet in pleasantly warm water can be a quick, easy alternative to a bath. If you can soak them in a whirlpool or spa-type foot bath, all the better. If you wish, add Epsom salts or your favorite aromatherapy oil. The warm water gently stimulates acupressure points on the soles of your feet and helps to circulate chi to the related parts of your body.

Stroke an animal companion.

Studies have shown that stroking a pet can measurably reduce stress and have a positive effect on many health conditions. The unconditional love animals give us is a wonderful tonic for body, mind, and spirit.

Wear silk.

Mystics and magicians often wrap their special tools in silk to protect them from ambient vibrations and unwanted energies. You can protect yourself from "bad vibes" in your environment by wearing silk garments.

Wear clothing made of natural fibers.

Evidence suggests that clothing made of natural fibers may be healthier than synthetics. Organic materials that are either unbleached or colored with natural dyes are considered beneficial—especially for sensitive people—because they don't impart any chemical byproducts to your body. Wool, cotton, silk, and other natural materials also retain some of the positive vibrations from their plant or animal sources.

Sleep on silk sheets.

We spend a third of our lives sleeping. Silk sheets can help protect you from energetic imbalances while you sleep, so you rest better and feel rejuvenated when you awaken.

Use *acupressure to center your mind.*

Gently press the point located at the base of your nose in the small depression above your upper lip and hold it for about thirty seconds. Activating this acupressure point helps to clear and center your mind. It can also let you release unwanted thoughts and enhance memory.

Use *acupressure to relieve anxiety*.

Your solar plexus, located about halfway between the bottom of your breastbone and your navel, is an emotional center. To release distressing feelings and relieve anxiety, gently press this spot for about thirty seconds. Activating this acupressure point also helps you balance mind and body.

Use *acupressure to calm nervousness and fears*.

On the outside of each forearm, at the spot where your hand and wrist join, are acupressure points that can be pressed to help calm fears and nervousness. Hold these points for about thirty seconds to balance emotions and produce a quiet, still, reflective mental state.

Press your thumbs and index fingers together.

Perhaps you've seen people doing this when they meditate. That's because the fingertips contain acupressure points that are linked with the brain. Pressing them helps to induce an alpha state—it can also let you tap into the intuitive portion of the mind and the subconscious. The next time you want to relax or spark your creativity, press your thumbs and index fingers together for about thirty seconds.

Give yourself a hug.

Cross your arms over your chest and grab your shoulders. Hold this position for about fifteen seconds. Then, open your arms as wide as you can. Inhale as you open your arms, exhale as you hug yourself. Repeat ten times. This exercise loosens and stretches the muscles in your arms, shoulders, and upper back. It also opens your lungs and allows you to breathe more deeply and fully.

Hug a friend.

We can all use a hug now and again. Hug a friend or loved one and focus all your attention on the other person while you share a caring embrace. Try to feel your chi interacting with your friend's chi, so that you support and enhance each other's energy fields.

Avoid elective medical procedures when Mercury is retrograde.

The planet Mercury goes retrograde every four months for about three weeks. During these weeks, it appears to be moving backwards in its orbit. (Consult an ephemeris, an astrologer, or online service to see when these periods are in effect.) Astrologers connect Mercury with the conscious mind and communication. When its motion is retrograde, confusion, lack of clarity, miscommunication, errors in judgment, and other mix-ups are likely to occur. Therefore, it's wise to avoid elective medical procedures during these periods. If you receive a disturbing or unclear result from a medical test that was taken while Mercury was retrograde, consider having the test redone. If you are unhappy with a doctor's prognosis, you may want to get a second opinion. If you must have medical work done during Mercury's retrograde cycle, be sure to communicate very clearly with medical personnel, make certain you understand what is being done, and don't leave anything to chance.

Get plenty of exercise when Mars is influencing you.

As the planets move in their orbits, their positions influence us in predictable ways. The energy of Mars is very stimulating and can make you feel restless, irritable, and impatient. Physical exercise can help you utilize this planetary chi in a positive way and prevent excess stress. Consult an ephemeris or an astrologer to find out when the energies of the different planets will be affecting you. (See Chapter 2 for more information about cosmic chi.)

Don't diet when under the influence of Jupiter.

Because Jupiter is the planet of expansion and growth, you may have trouble losing weight while this planet is influencing you. You might actually gain weight, even though your diet and routine remain the same. On the positive side, Jupiter's beneficial energy usually reinforces your vitality and resistance to illness.

Start a diet during the waning moon.

The waning moon (the two weeks between full and new) is a time of decrease. If you begin a diet a day or so after the full moon, you put yourself in tune with cosmic forces and therefore have a better chance of losing weight. As the moon grows thinner, so will you.

End a bad habit while Saturn is influencing you.

Saturn is the planet of limitations and self-discipline. Its energy can help you eliminate a bad habit. Under Saturn's influence, your determination increases so you are more likely to stick with your plan until you accomplish your goal.

Enjoy a salt scrub.

Many spas offer salt scrubs, which coat the body with a paste-like solution of sea, Epsom, or other salts. This beauty treatment relaxes mind and body while it gently exfoliates the skin and stimulates circulation.

Sit in a whirlpool.

The hot water and agitation in a whirlpool bath relax your muscles so chi can flow freely in your body. Add a few drops of essential oil of lavender to the water to make your bath even more soothing and pleasant. (Note: Many whirlpool and hot tub manufacturers advise limited use—maybe only ten to twenty minutes at a time. Make sure to follow recommended guidelines.)

Take vitamin C to prevent infections.

Vitamin C, found in many fruits and vegetables, is an antioxidant that helps to cleanse the system. It also helps to reduce stress, nourish nerve and brain cells, maintain healthy blood, and provide resistance to infection. Vitamin C supplements can augment your diet and prevent a deficiency of this vital nutrient.

Take B vitamins to promote relaxation.

B vitamins can help to combat stress and encourage relaxation. Found in grains, nuts, brewers' yeast, and some meats, the B-complex vitamins provide a wide range of physical and mental health benefits. They repair body tissues, aid in the formation of brain and nerve substances, and help the body convert food into energy. Taking B-complex supplements can also help relieve stress and mild depression.

Take vitamin E to promote healthy blood and muscles.

Vitamin E, found in nuts, fish, and plant oils, maintains healthy blood vessels and helps the muscles utilize oxygen efficiently. This antioxidant also promotes healthy skin. When the body is deficient in vitamin E, chi suffers—vitality diminishes, muscles weaken, and apathy sets in.

Make love.

Making love is one of the best and most enjoyable ways to raise your energy level. It's also good exercise, and encourages deep breathing and improved circulation. Biologist and psychiatrist Wilhelm Reich believed lovemaking was essential for optimal health because it stimulated the flow of orgone (chi) through the entire body. Some mystical sex practices, such as tantra, activate and direct the flow of chi through the chakras to energize, balance, and nourish the entire system.

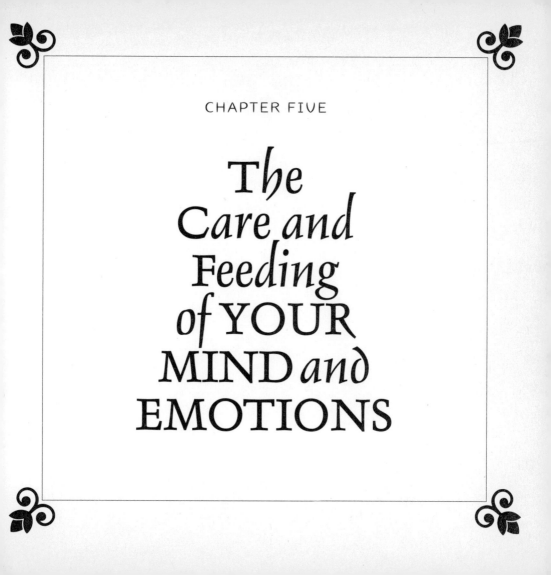

CHAPTER FIVE

The Care and Feeding of YOUR MIND and EMOTIONS

*t*he mind plays an integral role in physical health and well-being. The emotions also impact chi. Tips in this chapter are designed to help you balance your emotions and tap the power of your mind to facilitate overall health and happiness.

Meditate.

Meditation is one of the cornerstones of Eastern medical philosophy. An estimated million or so people in the U.S. now meditate daily. Those that do tend to enjoy both mental and physical health benefits, including reduced blood pressure, lower incidents of cardiac disease, stroke, and cancer. Meditating only ten minutes per day can have a positive impact on your chi. Whether you chant a mantra, concentrate on your breathing, or just sit quietly without thinking, meditation reduces stress and helps to balance the flow of chi through your body.

Pray.

One of the most obvious benefits of prayer is that it induces relaxation, just as meditation does. Consequently, praying can have a positive effect on chi. Blood pressure drops, heart rate slows, the breathing rate is lowered, the adrenal glands secrete fewer of the stress-response hormones. The system starts rejuvenating itself. Even serious and chronic illnesses often show marked improvement as a result of prayer, as the work of Larry Dossey and others have shown. There is no right or wrong way to pray. You can pray to God, the Goddess, a Divine Spirit, the All-knowing Power of the Universe, your guardian angel, the Ancestors—whatever presence you feel is guiding your life. A few minutes a day can enhance your overall sense of well-being—even work miracles.

Visualize chi flowing smoothly through your body.

The work of Shakti Gawain and other pioneers in the field of creative visualization have demonstrated the positive effects visualization can have on health and well-being. You can improve the flow of chi through your body by using your mind. Sit quietly, close your eyes, and bring to mind a picture of your body's meridian system. Imagine chi moving smoothly and harmoniously through those channels in your legs, arms, trunk, and head. If that's too complex, simply envision life energy flowing into your left foot, traveling up your leg and through your torso, out your arms to your fingertips, into your neck and head, then moving down your body again and out your right foot. Repeat this visualization several times each day to strengthen and balance your chi.

Visualize chi entering your body's acupuncture points.

A chart of the body's meridians and acupuncture points can be useful in this exercise, to show you where these entry points are located. Otherwise, simply envision dozens of tiny openings in your body where chi can enter. Lie down in a comfortable spot with your eyes closed. Imagine you are surrounded by a ball of pure white light that represents the life force. As you inhale, draw this life-giving energy into the acupuncture points all along your body. As you exhale, imagine it circulating through the meridians, carrying nourishment and vitality to every cell. Spend about five minutes each day performing this exercise in order to increase the amount of healthy chi in your system.

Visualize chi entering your body with each breath.

We derive chi from the air we breathe. To enhance the amount and quality of this life-giving chi, sit quietly and close your eyes. Envision pure white energy moving into your lungs each time you inhale. Imagine the chi circulating through your body, providing nourishment to every cell. As you exhale, envision impurities leaving your body.

Balance your root chakra.

The root chakra is situated near the base of your spine. This energy center is linked with feelings of security, survival, and connectedness. When this chakra is operating properly, chi flows through it easily to energize your system. Sit in a comfortable place with your back straight. Close your eyes. Imagine a ball of warm red light radiating in this area, removing any blockages that might exist there so that chi can move through it and bring vital energy into your body. (For more information about the chakras, see Chapter 3.)

Balance your sacral chakra.

The sacral chakra is situated near your abdomen, about three inches below your belly button. This energy center is connected with creativity and sexual vitality. To help keep chi flowing properly through this chakra, sit in a comfortable place with your back straight. Close your eyes. Imagine a ball of warm orange light radiating in this area, removing any blockages that might exist there so that chi can energize it and flow through it to other parts of your body.

Balance your solar plexus chakra.

This chakra is situated in your solar plexus, about three finger widths above your belly button. This energy center is connected with the emotions, will, and feelings of self-worth. To help keep chi flowing properly through this chakra, sit in a comfortable place with your back straight. Close your eyes. Imagine a ball of golden-yellow light, like the sun, radiating in this area. This warm, clear light removes any blockages that might exist there so that chi can energize the chakra and flow through it to other parts of your body.

Balance your heart chakra.

This chakra is situated near your heart. This center is associated with love and joy, and also serves to regulate the movement of energy from the lower to the upper part of your body. To help keep chi flowing properly through this chakra, sit in a comfortable place with your back straight. Close your eyes. Imagine a ball of green light, like spring grass, glowing in this area, removing any blockages that might exist there so that chi can energize it and flow through it to other parts of your body.

Balance your throat chakra.

This chakra is situated at the base of your neck, near the hollow between your collarbones. This center is linked with your ability to speak your own truth and to ask for what you want in life. To help keep chi flowing properly through this chakra, sit in a comfortable place with your back straight. Close your eyes. Imagine a ball of bright blue light glowing in this area, removing any blockages that might exist there so that chi can energize it and flow through it to other parts of your body.

Balance your brow chakra.

The brow chakra is situated on your forehead between your eyebrows, in the place we sometimes call the "third eye." This center is linked with your intuition. To help keep chi flowing properly through this chakra, sit in a comfortable place with your back straight. Close your eyes. Imagine a ball of indigo light glowing in this area, removing any blockages that might exist there so that chi can energize it and flow through it to other parts of your body.

Balance your crown chakra.

This chakra is situated at the top of your head. It is associated with your spiritual nature and your ability to connect with the Divine Source. To help keep chi flowing properly through this chakra, sit in a comfortable place with your back straight. Close your eyes. Imagine a ball of purple light glowing in this area, removing any blockages that might exist there, so that chi can energize it and enhance your sense of yourself as part of the cosmic order.

Visualize chi moving up your spine.

Sit in a comfortable place with your back straight. Close your eyes. As you inhale, imagine chi flowing up from the center of the earth, into the base of your spine. Visualize this life energy moving up your spine and, as you exhale, see it spouting from the top of your head, like water in a fountain, showering you with vitality. Repeat this mental exercise several times each day to keep chi moving freely through your spine. This visualization technique also helps to harmonize the seven main chakras.

Ask a friend to direct chi up your spine.

Ask a friend to stand behind you and hold his/her hand a few inches away from the lower part of your back, near your root chakra. Your friend's palm should be facing your body. As you inhale, ask your friend to move his/her hand up your spine to the top of your head, without actually touching your physical body. Imagine chi rising in your spine as your friend's hand moves up. When your friend's hand reaches the top of your head, exhale slowly. Repeat this exercise several times to activate your chi and distribute it evenly through your body. Then, switch places and use your hand to activate your friend's chi.

Strengthen your "sea of energy."

This spot, located just below your navel and slightly toward your back, is a center of balance in the body. Stand or sit comfortably and hold your hands slightly cupped, with your palms facing inward toward this part of your body. If you wish, you can hold one hand in front of your abdomen and the other hand opposite it near the small of your back. Close your eyes and imagine chi flowing from your palms into this energy center. Feel the chi mixing and harmonizing in your sea of energy, until your body feels centered and balanced.

Activate a spiral of energy.

The spiral is an ancient symbol for life energy. Sit with your back straight, your feet flat on the floor, and your eyes closed. Take a few slow, deep breaths, inhaling and exhaling completely. Hold your left hand open a few inches in front of your body with your palm turned in toward your stomach or solar plexus. Sense the energy between your solar plexus and your palm. If necessary, move your hand closer or further away from your stomach, until you feel a slight "touch" even though your hand doesn't physically touch your body. Begin making slow clockwise circles with your hand. As you do this, sense the movement of the energy you are stirring up. Continue circulating the chi in your solar plexus for a minute or so, until you activate the vital energy situated there.

Think positive thoughts upon awakening.

The first thoughts you have in the morning affect the rest of your day. As soon as you wake up, think of something positive and healing. Don't start the day by worrying about all the chores or problems that await you. Each morning, take this opportunity to encourage health, happiness, and good fortune by holding a positive thought in your mind for a few moments.

Avoid self-deprecating statements.

Often, we carelessly chastise ourselves with insulting statements such as "How could I be so stupid" or "What a klutz I am" or "I look awful." Stop saying hurtful things to yourself. Self-deprecating comments like this have a damaging effect on your sense of self and undermine your happiness, success, and well-being.

Turn off your inner chatter.

This is more difficult than it sounds, for our minds constantly carry on a running inner dialogue, jumping from one thought to another. Sit quietly and focus your mind on your breathing. Really pay attention to each inhalation and exhalation, the movement of breath through your body, and the sensations that accompany breathing. Each time your mind starts to wander, gently pull it back to your breath and release whatever thoughts were interrupting your concentration. Do this for a few minutes each day to reduce stress and improve mental focus.

Practice forgiveness.

Many spiritual leaders and holistic healers teach that forgiveness is essential to health and happiness. Holding on to anger, grievances, disappointments, resentment, and fears can cause disturbances in your vital energy field and in some cases lead to physical problems. Forgive yourself and others for their shortcomings. If you cannot do this face-to-face, write a letter to the person you wish to forgive (even if you never mail it). Or, call this person's image to you while you are meditating and mentally forgive him or her.

Create a calming mental image.

Stress has a damaging effect on chi and can lead to blockages, imbalances, and other energetic upsets—even physical illness. Create a soothing image to help you cope with stress. This might be a picture of an actual place you know or one you create in your imagination. You might think of waves gently breaking on a beach, taking a walk in the woods, or sitting in a lush meadow surrounded by wildflowers on a sunny day. Whenever you feel stress mounting, stop and recall your peaceful image. Hold this image in your mind for a few moments until you feel the tension begin to subside.

Focus on one thing at a time.

Most of us let our minds jump about from one thing to another, rarely holding a single thought for more than a few seconds. While we're doing one thing, we're usually thinking about something else. This sort of mental juggling can be very stressful, however. Train yourself to focus on the task at hand and to devote all your attention to it—even if it's a seemingly mindless chore like washing dishes or raking leaves. Thinking about one thing at a time helps to center the mind and quiet the emotions.

Inhale peppermint essential oil to clear your mind.

As the art of aromatherapy has shown, scents affect the limbic system of the brain and can produce measurable results very quickly. To clear your mind and improve concentration, put a few drops of peppermint essential oil on a handkerchief and inhale the aroma. Or, burn mint incense to open up your thinking processes and stimulate the flow of energy to the brain. (See Chapter 3 for more information.)

Inhale lavender essential oil to calm your mind.

When inhaled, the lovely scent of lavender quickly soothes the mind and emotions. If you are under stress or are having trouble sleeping, put a few drops of lavender essential oil on a handkerchief and breathe deeply to calm nerves, mental restlessness, and tension. If you prefer, burn lavender incense or a lavender-scented candle. You can also add lavender essential oil to a hot bath or combine it with massage oil. Or, mist bed linens lightly with lavender-scented water.

Inhale essential oil of sweet orange to chase away the blues.

The oil of the fruit of this evergreen tree acts as a mild antidepressant. When you're feeling down, counteract unhappiness with this pleasing and uplifting scent. Mix a few drops in a base of olive or grapeseed oil and dab it on your wrists, or dot a handkerchief with pure essential oil and inhale the delicious aroma to chase the blues away.

Inhale vanilla essential oil to improve self-esteem.

The warm, mellow scent of vanilla can engender feelings of comfort, relaxation, and security, according to studies done at Memorial-Sloan Kettering Cancer Center in New York. If you are experiencing mild anxiety or a lack of self-confidence, rub a little of this calming essential oil on your wrists and inhale it to enhance your self-esteem. If you prefer, burn a vanilla-scented candle or vanilla incense.

Take St. John's wort to elevate your emotions.

This herb is a mild tranquilizer and mood elevator that can relieve mild depression, anxiety, and insomnia. Many people who suffer from Seasonal Affective Disorder during the winter benefit from taking St. John's wort.

Cleanse your chi with green light.

Green is the color of plants. Vibrational healers often associate this soothing color with growth and health, because it is at the midpoint of the visible color spectrum. To cleanse and rejuvenate chi, especially during times of stress, anxiety, or illness, close your eyes and imagine your body surrounded by a ball of clear green light. As you inhale, visualize this light flowing into your lungs and circulating through your body. As you exhale, see all the imbalances, toxins, and impurities leaving your system with your breath. Repeat this exercise for about one minute to help cleanse your chi.

Strengthen your chi with golden light.

Gold is the color of the sun—a color you can use to strengthen your chi and your overall vitality. Close your eyes and imagine your body surrounded by a ball of shimmering golden light. As you inhale, visualize this light flowing into your lungs and circulating through your body. As you exhale, see all the imbalances, toxins, and impurities leaving your system with your breath. Repeat this exercise for about one minute to help revitalize your chi.

Protect yourself with white light.

Whenever you feel a need for a little extra protection, close your eyes and imagine your body surrounded by a ball of pure white light. As you inhale, visualize this light flowing into your lungs and circulating through your body. As you exhale, see all the imbalances, fears, and worries leaving your system with your breath. Repeat this exercise for about one minute to protect yourself from physical, psychic, or other harm.

Bathe yourself in pink light.

Pink is the color of love, so this color can help you strengthen your self-esteem or eliminate anger that can disrupt the flow of chi through your system. Close your eyes and imagine your body surrounded by a ball of beautiful rosy-pink light. As you inhale, visualize this light flowing into your lungs and circulating through your body. As you exhale, see all the disruptions, worries, and fears leaving your system with your breath. Repeat this exercise for about one minute to help balance your chi.

Take a chi shower.

Stand with your hands above your head, palms facing up toward the sky, and visualize yourself drawing chi down from the heavens. When you have collected this cosmic chi, turn your hands so your palms face your head. Imagine the chi you've collected is now raining down on your head, like an energy shower. Slowly, draw your hands down in front of your body, holding your palms a few inches away and facing in so they direct the flow of chi toward you. Then, do the same thing to your back, focusing chi toward your body. Perform this technique whenever you need a "pick-me-up" or when you feel stressed out and want to calm and balance your chi.

Read inspirational literature.

The *Tao Te Ching, I Ching,* the poems of Rumi, and many other spiritual or inspirational texts offer uplifting food for thought. Take a few minutes in the morning or before going to sleep at night to nourish your mind with positive words of wisdom.

Read Zen koans.

Koans are devices designed to stimulate contemplation. Some koans are baffling questions, others may be stories or metaphorical situations whose meanings seem ambiguous or confusing. One of the most famous koans is "What is the sound of one hand clapping?" Koans cannot be understood with the rational, analytical mind—they speak to a deeper part of us. A koan's objective is to frustrate the mind until it "gives up" and allows the intuition or "inner knowing" to unravel the conundrum. Then truth emerges.

Read haiku.

Traditional haiku poems contain three lines and seventeen syllables. The first and last lines generally describe stable conditions, while the middle line interjects a changing or transient image. Nature is often a central theme in haiku, and the concepts presented tend to be deceptively simple. Both the subject matter and the rhythm of haiku poems can relax your mind and inspire feelings of serenity.

Pay attention to moon cycles.

The moon's twenty-eight-day cycle has a profound effect on your emotions. As the moon travels through the zodiac, it remains in each astrological sign for about two and one-half days. While it occupies a particular sign, you experience some of the energy of that sign. For example, you might feel more vigorous when the moon is in Aries and more introspective when it is in Pisces. Start paying attention to the moon's influence on your mental and emotional states. Aligning yourself and your activities with the position of the moon can help you become more balanced, content, and productive. You may even improve your health.

Repeat a positive affirmation frequently.

Affirmations are positive statements that you say to yourself to encourage certain attitudes, behavior, or conditions. When you repeat an affirmation, you give your subconscious instructions to carry out. Ideally, an affirmation should be stated in the present tense and be short and to the point. For example, you could repeat this affirmation to improve your chi: "Every day in every way I am becoming healthier and happier." You may also wish to write your affirmation on a piece of paper and display it in a place where you will see it often.

Create an energy-balancing incantation.

An incantation is a short, simple rhyme or poem that contains a positive message or intention. Similar to an affirmation, an incantation is repeated frequently to "program" your subconscious and to produce a desired condition. For instance, you might say something like: "Life-giving energy flows through me/I am blessed with healthy chi." Repeat your incantation frequently to encourage mind-body harmony.

Choose a personal mantra.

Many people repeat mantras during meditation to help them focus their minds and center themselves. The resonating sound of a mantra, such as *om* (intoned slowly *aahooommm*), can also have a calming, rejuvenating effect on the body. You can benefit from saying a mantra even when you aren't engaged in meditation. During times of stress, for instance, repeat a word that has meaning for you such as *relax, release, serenity*, or *tranquility.*

Coordinate a mantra with your breathing.

A mantra may be coordinated with your breathing to amplify its positive effects. *Om,* for instance, is usually intoned as you exhale. If you prefer, you can choose a two-word mantra that has meaning for you and hold it in your mind as you breathe, rather than saying it aloud. For example, I often think the word "live" as I inhale and "love" as I exhale. Try thinking "relax" as you inhale and "release" as you exhale to reduce stress.

Don't dwell on what you lack.

Focusing on what you lack or on your problems tends to exacerbate them and increase their importance in your life. Some schools of thought hold that you actually attract whatever you focus your attention on. Instead of dwelling on unpleasant thoughts, discipline your mind and keep it centered on positive, harmonious things.

Count your blessings.

When life's challenges weigh on you, it helps to remember the many good things in your life—good health, loving friends, hobbies, and so on. Make a list of ten (or more) blessings you enjoy and read it each morning. Counting your blessings can lift your spirits and keep your mind focused on positive thoughts.

Get some sunshine every day.

Seasonal Affective Disorder, a common type of depression with the apt acronym SAD, is connected with the annual reduction of sunlight in northern latitudes. Between 5 and 10 percent of the entire U.S. population and more than 20 percent of those living in the northern parts of the country—perhaps as many as 35 million people—experience some degree of SAD. Some people are so severely affected by light deprivation that they lapse into full-scale depression during the dark days of winter. The best way to cope with SAD is to be exposed to sunlight for at least ten minutes every day. When that isn't possible, use a light box or full-spectrum lights, which contain the entire visible and invisible ends of the color spectrum, including ultraviolet and infrared light.

Contemplate the yin/yang symbol.

This symbol represents the interrelationship of yin and yang, the universal feminine and masculine energies. Contemplating this image can help to balance yin and yang forces within yourself. If you wish, display the symbol in a place where you will see it often. In times of stress, take a few moments to gaze at the symbol and balance yourself. (See Chapter 2 for more about yin and yang.)

Create a chi-balancing mandala.

Mandala means circle in Sanskrit. Usually painted or drawn, mandalas can be created in just about any medium—permanent or temporary. Often a mandala contains mystical or magical symbolism designed to influence those who look at it on a subconscious level. Many mandalas are divided into two hemispheres—earth and sky—and include representations of the four elements. Thus, they convey a sense of balance and unity. Tibetan Buddhists use mandalas as tools for meditation and contemplation. Mandalas can also be found in the rose windows of Europe's great cathedrals, in Oriental rugs, and in nature. You can design and fabricate your own mandala to help balance your chi and facilitate emotional harmony. (For more about mandalas, see my book *Magickal Astrology*.)

Try your hand at sand painting.

Sand painting, a technique practiced by Buddhist monks and some American Indian tribes, is both a form of meditation and magic. Because sand painting requires skill and care, you must focus your attention completely on the task at hand. But you can't get too invested in a sand painting—its very nature is transient. Thus, this creative process can help you calm and center yourself, discipline your mind, and let go of your attachments to the physical world.

Rake a Zen garden.

Some Zen practices involve seemingly mundane tasks—such as raking a garden—as exercises in spiritual development. These practices enable you to slow down, focus your mind, and center yourself by paying attention to a simple, repetitious chore. You don't have to rake a full-size garden—miniature, tabletop versions complete with sand, stones, and rake are available. When you feel stressed or upset, take a few minutes to calm your mind by running a rake peacefully through the sand.

Avoid mental stress while Mercury is retrograde.

Every four months for three weeks at a time, the planet Mercury turns retrograde. During these periods, your analytical and communication skills take a back seat to your intuition and imagination. This is a good time to shift your focus from outer-directed, rational thinking and tasks that demand mental clarity. Instead, devote more time to introspection and rest. (See Chapter 2 for more information.)

Go on retreat while Mercury is retrograde.

If possible, take time off from your usual schedule while
Mercury is retrograde. Go on retreat or take a vacation. During this
period, your conscious mind doesn't work as clearly or quickly as usual,
and trying to push yourself is likely to produce adverse results such
as stress, confusion, and mistakes. Instead of focusing on rational,
analytical tasks, turn your attention to inner-oriented practices such
as meditation, reflection, using your intuition, and creative pursuits.

Pay attention to your dreams.

Dreams are one of the ways your subconscious and your higher self communicate with you. Often dreams provide information that can guide you in your waking life. Your dreams may even alert you to problems with health or other important issues that need attention. If you have trouble remembering your dreams, tell yourself each night as you lie down to sleep that upon awakening you *will* recall what you've dreamt. Keep a dream journal to encourage dream recollection and to become familiar with your own dream symbols.

CHAPTER SIX

The Care and Feeding of YOUR SPIRIT

*t*ips and techniques in this chapter are designed to uplift your spirit and promote an overall sense of well-being. Some of the therapies included here work on the subtle energy bodies to balance chi and support good health at a spiritual level.

Observe silence for ten minutes each day.

Many spiritual traditions advocate silence as a way of tuning out the stress and distractions of the everyday world, so you can connect with your own inner being and the Divine. In our fast-paced, hectic world, silence is rare—and it can be very healing. Set aside time each day to be alone and quiet. For ten minutes, don't do anything, just sit and enjoy being still, silent, and serene. If you wish, go to a peaceful place—a garden, park, or pleasant room in your home—where you won't be disturbed and can rest and relax. Notice any insights or revelations that present themselves to you during this period and write them down when you emerge from your self-imposed "silent retreat."

Live in the moment.

The present is the only time we can do anything about—the past is over and the future is yet to come. Yet most of us spend a good deal of each day worrying about both the past and future while the present slips by unnoticed. This sort of planning and rehashing can also be stressful and disconcerting, because "control" of the past and future is out of your hands. In order to fully experience each moment, it's necessary to pay attention to the here and now. Discipline your mind so it doesn't continually flit from thought to thought. Paying attention to what's going on right now can enrich your appreciation of life and encourage serenity.

Do something you love each day.

Too often, we devote our time and energy to chores, responsibilities, and obligations while neglecting the things that make our hearts sing. Studies show, however, that happiness is an important factor in maintaining good health. Set aside a block of time each day to do something you love, that brings meaning and joy into your life.

Get a Reiki treatment.

Reiki is a word for universal energy, or chi, although it is generally used to describe the therapy itself. Reiki healers serve as conduits for universal chi and direct it into a patient whose chi is deficient or unbalanced. This energy-harmonizing therapy links you with the source of universal chi and optimizes the flow of chi through your body. (See Chapter 3 for more information.)

Get a Polarity treatment.

Polarity therapy balances the flow of chi through the body's main energy centers, known as the chakras. To improve chi's function in your body and keep your chakras operating harmoniously, get a Polarity treatment. (See Chapter 3 for more information.)

Take time to smell the flowers.

The great Austrian mystic Rudolf Steiner taught that observing flowers and other living things closely—not just with your eyes, but with your heart—was an essential part of a person's training on the path to enlightenment. Steiner recommended focusing all your attention on plants during their growth and blossoming stages, then during their dying and fading away phases. While doing this, pay attention to the feelings and insights that arise in connection with your observations. These feelings and impressions help to awaken and elevate your higher sensibilities as well as nurturing your spiritual connection to the Source.

Listen to the birds sing.

Steiner also suggested listening carefully to bird sounds as part of your spiritual development. By sensitizing yourself to the world around you and the other beings who share our planet with us, you increase your awareness of the interconnectedness of all life. This awareness can also produce feelings of peace and balance.

Use flower remedies.

Flower remedies are derived from the vital essence of various plants, but contain no actual plant material. Each flower, tree, or other plant possesses certain characteristics that can be useful in treating specific problems in humans and animals. The plant's vibrations interact with your subtle bodies to adjust and balance disturbances in your energy field, ultimately affecting your emotions, thoughts, and/or physical condition. (See Chapter 3 for more information.)

Let the essence of elm help you handle responsibilities.

When you feel overburdened by life's demands or have taken on too much, this tree essence can help you handle responsibilities and avoid burn-out.

Take Star of Bethlehem to help soothe stress.

After a trauma that upsets your system, take essence of the Star of Bethlehem. This flower remedy helps soothe stress and restores psychic and emotional balance.

Take Indian Pink to stay centered.

This flower remedy can help you keep your cool in the midst of intense activity. When life gets too hectic, let Indian Pink restore your sense of calm and serenity.

Take hornbeam to increase energy.

If you feel listless, for no obvious physical or emotional reason, this flower remedy can help lift your spirits and improve your energy.

Take impatiens to help you remain calm.

If you are inclined to be impatient with yourself or others, this flower remedy can help you slow down. In times of stress, essence of impatiens can help you stay calm and centered.

Take bleeding heart to heal a broken heart.

The pain that comes from losing a loved one, whether through death or separation, is among the most devastating and disruptive emotions. Both people and animals have been known to die from broken hearts, and all sorts of illnesses—from colds to cancer—can be linked to the destructive effect of grief. Essence of bleeding heart works on the subtle energy bodies to help relieve this profound pain and restore balance on a spiritual as well as an emotional level.

Take borage to increase joy.

This flower remedy helps to relieve sadness and lift the heart. It can also restore confidence and courage. When you feel disheartened or discouraged, take borage to increase optimism and joy.

Take Rescue Remedy when you feel exhausted.

This popular blend of flower essences helps to counteract the energy-draining effects of shock, trauma, stress, mental and emotional exhaustion.

Light a candle.

Candles symbolize the sun's life-giving light. They also play a role in many rituals and spiritual practices, where they represent hope, positive energy, and spirit. In feng shui, candles are used to augment the fire element and yang energy. Gaze into the candle's flame and let your mind and body relax. When you are calm and centered, chi can move more freely and harmoniously through your body.

Burn scented candles.

When you burn candles scented with pure essential oils, you combine two techniques to uplift your spirit and balance your chi. The symbolism of fire has a positive influence on your psyche, while the aromatherapy benefits of the essential oils trigger responses in your mind. Choose a scent that matches your intention. (Note: Many candles are perfumed with synthetic fragrances, which don't possess the healing properties of real essential oils.)

Seek Divine assistance.

Human understanding and perception are necessarily limited, but Divine wisdom is infinite. Ask whatever higher power you recognize—God, Goddess, Higher Self, Ancestor, Guardian Angel—to guide you. When you seek Divine assistance with sincerity and for the good of all concerned, miracles can happen. Remember to offer thanks for this assistance.

Turn your problems over to a higher power.

Sometimes the challenges in our lives seem too big to handle ourselves. If you feel overwhelmed by a problem or just don't know how to handle a difficult situation, consciously hand it over to a higher power. Then step back, release the problem, stop worrying, and allow Divine assistance to resolve matters for the good of all concerned.

Trust.

The *I Ching* and many other spiritual texts urge us to trust, even when faced with difficult challenges. Fear and doubt interfere with the creative work of the Divine. If you have sought guidance or assistance from a higher power, trust that you will receive the help you need in the correct way at the correct time.

Practice acceptance.

The *I Ching,* a 3,000-year-old oracle and book of Chinese wisdom supposedly written by Confucius, recommends letting go of preconceived expectations and ego demands. When we hold expectations—of ourselves or others—the pressure of our desires produces stress and resistance. Other people may balk (inwardly or outwardly) because our demands deprive them of the privilege of exercising their own free will. If our expectations aren't met, we are likely to feel disappointed. We may also miss out on opportunities and joys that weren't within the scope of our fixed ideas.

Listen to music.

It's been said that music soothes the savage breast. Playing classical music to plants can actually enhance their growth (see *The Secret Life of Plants* by Peter Tompkins for details). Listening to soothing or uplifting music can have a positive effect on human beings, too. The works of Mozart, Bach, and Vivaldi are good for balancing your energy fields. Some "new age" musicians compose pieces for meditation, harmonizing the chakras, uplifting the spirit, or connecting with the Divine. Gerald Jay Markoe's compositions even help you get in touch with cosmic energies.

Enjoy art.

Great art is more than mere decoration—it speaks to the soul and uplifts the spirit. You don't have to be a connoisseur to enjoy art. Observing compositions that embody the principles of spatial balance and color harmony can soothe and regulate your chi. Some artwork even contains mystical and magical symbols that represent universal truths; when you look at them, their energy patterns are imprinted on your subconscious.

Watch the sunrise or sunset.

Whenever possible, pause to watch the sunrise or sunset—the universe's awe-inspiring light shows—and enjoy a few minutes of relaxation. In these peaceful moments, you can connect with nature and the diurnal cycles that give order to our lives.

Enjoy a rainbow.

Rainbows are ancient symbols of hope. As sunlight and clarity break through after a storm, gaze at a rainbow to lift your spirits and renew your optimism.

Hold a piece of quartz crystal.

Healers who use gemstones in their work believe that genuine quartz crystal has the power to amplify the energy of other stones and substances. It can also strengthen, protect, and purify your own energy field. Hold or wear a piece of pure quartz crystal to attract positive, healing vibrations and to help shield you from unwanted ambient vibrations that might disturb your personal chi. (Note: Make sure to cleanse crystals before using them by running them under water and visualizing them surrounded and suffused by white light.)

Hold a piece of smoky quartz to release worries.

Smoky quartz has a grayish cast and is believed by crystal workers to possess special powers of retention and memory. This concept isn't so strange when you think that quartz is used in watches and other devices that store data. If you feel burdened by worries, hold a piece of smoky quartz to your forehead or heart and imagine you are unloading your problems into the quartz temporarily. The smoky quartz crystal will accept and store your worries until you feel better equipped to retrieve and deal with them.

Hold a piece of rose quartz to promote balance.

Lovely rose quartz is prized for its gentle vibrations. Holding it can encourage feelings of love, peace, and harmony. When you feel anxious, insecure, or sad, wear or carry a piece of rose quartz in your pocket and touch it often to help balance your emotions and lift your spirits.

Hold *a piece of amethyst to encourage serenity.*

Since ancient times, amethysts have been linked with peace and balance. This stone's soothing vibrations can help restore a sense of calm and harmony when you feel upset, restless, or irritable. Some people find amethyst relieves anxiety and helps them sleep better. If stress and discord threaten to upset your tranquility, hold or wear an amethyst and rub it whenever you start to feel tense.

Hold *a piece of onyx to ground your energy.*

The energy of onyx is so dense and focused that it can help you ground your own energy. To connect with the stabilizing vibrations in this gemstone, hold or wear a large piece of onyx. When your mind starts to wander, touch the stone and let it bring you back to the present.

Hold *a piece of citrine to cleanse your energy.*

Golden citrine serves as a cleansing agent for energy fields. After an upsetting experience or a period of stress, hold or wear a piece of citrine to remove disturbances in your chi and realign your life force. Citrine can also be used to cleanse the vibrational properties of your other crystals and gemstones.

Protect yourself with amber.

Amber isn't actually a stone—it's hardened sap. This lovely golden substance has long been valued for its protective properties. The vibrations it emits can shield you from physical or psychic disturbances and help alert you to potential dangers. Wear or carry a piece of amber when you travel or if you feel a need for a little extra protection.

Create a personal ritual.

Rituals help to anchor our lives. Rituals also allow us to remove ourselves temporarily from ordinary time and space, immersing ourselves in a period of reverence outside of our everyday routines. All cultures create their own meaningful rituals—sacred and secular—to celebrate themselves, their deities, and their way of life. You can establish your own personal ritual to honor whatever you value. Or, simply create a ritual that allows you time and space to reflect, relax, and center yourself.

CHAPTER SEVEN

Healing Chi in YOUR ENVIRONMENT

*C*hi flows through the land, the cosmos, and our environments. Feng shui's goal is to manipulate chi in the environment so that it benefits us on every level. Environmental chi has a profound impact on our personal chi, our health, and our overall sense of well-being. Simultaneously, our activities affect earth and cosmic chi. The tips and techniques in this chapter include feng shui cures as well as suggestions for tapping into environmental chi to promote personal health and happiness.

Clean up clutter in your home.

From the perspective of feng shui, physical clutter in your living environment symbolizes messiness in your personal life. If an area in your home is cluttered, you'll probably experience confusion or blockages in the part of your life that corresponds to the cluttered section. Conversely, areas that you just naturally tend to keep neat and organized show the parts of your life that function smoothly. Chi moves through your home in much the same way you do—if you must walk around piles of magazines, toys, sports equipment, clothes, tools, or other obstacles, chi will have a difficult time flowing smoothly through your living space. By clearing away clutter and obstructions, you enable chi to move freely and fill your home with positive, life-giving energy. (For more information, see my book, *10-Minute Clutter Control.*)

Clean up clutter in your workplace.

Clutter in your work area represents confusion, disorganization, obstacles, and lack of clarity in your professional life. When clutter in your workplace prevents chi from moving about freely, your business may languish, finances can suffer, and communication problems might occur. Clear up clutter in your work environment to encourage the healthy flow of chi or to revitalize your business.

Clean up the area near your home.

Accumulated trash, dead leaves, and other debris make the area around your home unsightly—they can also interfere with the smooth flow of chi to your home. Clear away this clutter so that chi in the environment can easily reach your home and bring its blessings into your life.

Fix cracked or broken pavement in a driveway or sidewalk.

Like many feng shui cures, this one has both a practical side and a symbolic one. On the practical side, repairing a damaged sidewalk or driveway can prevent accidents. From a feng shui perspective, broken pavement, sagging steps, and other signs of disrepair interfere with the smooth flow of chi to your home—fix damage to invite external chi into your life.

Make sure the entrance to your home is clear and accessible.

Chi comes in through the doors of your home. A cluttered or obstructed entryway blocks this life-generating force and inhibits your health, wealth, and happiness. Visitors to your home get their first impressions of you from your entrance, too. Make certain your front door, porch, and steps are neat, so that they speak well of you and are inviting to chi.

Install adequate lighting at your front door.

Light symbolizes the sun's life-giving energy. In feng shui, light helps to attract positive chi and augments its vitalizing power. Install adequate lighting at the entrance to your residence to draw environmental chi to your home. From a practical viewpoint, good lighting enables you and visitors to see clearly when entering your home, and can prevent accidents.

Hang a mirror on a door that faces a busy street.

If you live on a busy or noisy street, hang a mirror on the door facing the street to symbolically reflect noise and disruptive energy away from your home. This feng shui cure helps prevent outside irritations and stress from adversely impacting the inhabitants of your home.

Plant shrubs or trees between your home and a busy street.

This more permanent cure provides an attractive barrier between your home and the street. Physically and symbolically, plants absorb and block street noise and disruptive energies so they don't disturb the inhabitants of your home. This cure can also be used to screen an unpleasant view or as a buffer between your home and the potentially harmful electromagnetic fields (EMFs) generated by power lines.

Hang a wind chime between your home and electrical power lines.

To counteract the unwanted effects of EMFs from outdoor power lines, hang a wind chime between your home and the electrical lines. This cure helps to disperse stress-producing EMFs that can disrupt your well-being by circulating them away from your home.

Weed your garden.

Weeds suggest that problems are choking your personal growth and stifling your well-being. Pull them out to remove impediments to your health and happiness. Weeds also obscure flowers and deprive them of nutrients—get rid of them so you can showcase your favorite plants.

Clean gutters.

In feng shui, clogged gutters are symbols of stagnant conditions and obstructions in your life. Shui literally means "water." Ideally you want water in and around your home to flow in a smooth, gentle manner. When water becomes blocked, chi gets stuck. Clean out gutters so water—and chi—can flow freely.

Turn on the lights.

Low lighting may conserve electricity, but it can also diminish the life force in your home or workplace. In feng shui, light symbolizes the sun's life-giving energy and serves to increase positive chi. Especially in the winter, when natural sunlight is less abundant, turn on the lights and replace low-wattage bulbs with more powerful ones to boost beneficial chi. From a practical perspective, good lighting allows you to see where you're going and what you're doing, potentially increasing productivity and preventing accidents.

Replace burned out lights in your home and workplace.

Burned out light bulbs cut down on the amount of positive chi available to energize your home or business. They also represent areas in your personal or professional life that aren't functioning properly. Replace burned out lights in your home and workplace to enhance chi and light up your life.

Place a vase of fresh flowers in your entryway.

Flowers are not only an attractive accent in your home, they symbolize growth and life. Place these in your entrance area to attract good fortune and happiness. (Note: In feng shui, red is considered an auspicious color; so red flowers are thought to be especially lucky.)

Surround yourself with live plants.

Plants are one of the most common feng shui cures, because they represent life and growth. Plants also help to clean the air by absorbing carbon dioxide and releasing oxygen. Live plants serve as attractive and healthy accents in your home or workplace, and enhance the positive chi in your environment.

Trim houseplants.

Plants symbolize growth—keep yours neatly trimmed to encourage new growth in your life. Dry, brown leaves are not only unattractive, they represent death, decay, and stagnant conditions. Spindly vines suggest things are growing out of control and need to be reined in.

Tie bells to your doorknobs.

Pleasing sounds help to disperse unwanted ambient energies from the environment and break up stuck chi. Tie bells to your doorknobs so they tinkle when you open the doors in your home or work area. Or, place a bell near the entrance to each room so you can ring it whenever you go in or out.

Clear the walkways through your home.

Keep the walkways through your home free of furniture, clutter, and other obstructions. Can you move comfortably from one room to the next? Can you easily access windows and closets? Or do you have to sidestep walls, furnishing, or piles of clutter? Obstacles in your home's passageways block the smooth flow of chi and limit the life-enhancing benefits it brings.

Don't store stuff under your bed.

Clutter under your bed blocks the smooth flow of chi and may disrupt your sleep. Blocked chi can also produce confusion, obstacles, or stagnant conditions between you and a partner with whom you share a bed. If your living space is limited and you must utilize the area under your bed, be sure to neatly organize what you stash there. Pay attention to the symbolism attached to the items you place beneath your bed, too. Sharp objects, for instance, may produce subconscious feelings of discomfort that could disturb your sleep.

Walk a labyrinth.

Many people confuse labyrinths with mazes, but they aren't the same. Mazes are puzzles with lots of tricks and dead ends. Labyrinths have only one, winding path that leads into the center and back out again. For thousands of years, people all over the world have used labyrinths for mystical, magical, and meditative purposes. Walking a labyrinth helps to relax your mind and focus your attention. As you shift directions, you alternate between using the right brain and the left brain, activating both hemispheres so you feel balanced, calm, and centered. When you walk a labyrinth, you also connect with the chi in the land and strengthen your sense of oneness with the earth and cosmos.

Eliminate straight lines and sharp angles in a garden.

Gardens are oases where we go to find peace and relaxation. Straight lines and sharp angles, however, symbolize rapid movement and activity, and can produce stress instead of tranquility. Nature doesn't form straight lines or right angles—follow her lead and design your garden with graceful curves that encourage the smooth, calm flow of chi.

Hang prayer flags to promote peace.

Buddhists traditionally hang colorful flags printed with prayers and blessings outside their homes and temples. When the wind blows, it carries the blessings to all beings around the globe. You can write your own prayers and good wishes on colorful pieces of cloth and tie them on a pole, tree, or clothesline to promote peaceful, healing conditions in your environment and in the world.

Burn sage to clear bad vibes from your environment.

"Smudging" is a technique used to disperse bad vibes from your home to keep them from interfering with your health, wealth, or happiness. Clear the air by burning bundled white sage or sage incense to purify the space and remove unwanted ambient energies. Often used in preparation for ceremonies, rituals, or meditation, this practice is especially important when you move into a new home to remove the old chi left behind by previous occupants. Burning sage can also clear away unsettling vibrations after an argument or unpleasant event, or it can restore tranquility after a party or gathering in your home. It's also a good idea to smudge antiques and used furniture before bringing them into your living space.

Clean out your refrigerator.

Not only is spoiled food unhealthy, it clutters up your refrigerator. Cleaning out your refrigerator on a weekly basis makes it easier to find things, cuts down on waste, and prevents bacteria from building up. Because one of the main sources of chi is the food you eat, make sure your diet is as healthy as possible. Rework leftovers into soups, stews, or casseroles.

Clean your stove.

The Chinese believe the stove generates wealth and amplifies positive chi. Keep your stove clean and in good working order to encourage prosperity and well-being. Turn on your stove's burners briefly each day, even if you don't actually cook anything.

Wash windows.

In feng shui, windows symbolize the eyes. Clean windows allow you to see situations clearly. If you are experiencing confusion in a particular area of your life, wash windows in the part of your home that corresponds to that area to restore clarity and perspective. Chi also enters your home through the windows. Dirty or cracked windowpanes will hamper the flow of chi into your home and your life.

Empty wastebaskets daily.

Trash signifies old, cast-off stuff you no longer want or need. Empty wastebaskets daily to prevent "stuck" chi from building up in your home or workplace.

Repair or replace broken or damaged furnishings.

Much of feng shui involves symbolic associations. Physical conditions in our environments symbolize emotional issues and attitudes we hold. Broken furniture, for instance, can signify broken dreams, physical injuries, or a breakdown in communication among family members. In the workplace, broken objects may represent broken agreements or damage to your company's image. Repair or replace furnishings and equipment that are worn, damaged, or not working properly.

Fix doors and windows that don't open or close properly.

Chi enters your home or place of business through the doors and windows. If doors and windows stick or don't work properly, chi won't be able to come in easily. To facilitate chi's movement into and through your living and work spaces, make sure the doors and windows can be opened without difficulty. Whenever possible, leave interior doors open to encourage the smooth flow of chi through all parts of your home or work area.

Combine the four Western elements in your home.

To encourage balance and harmony in your home, include furnishings that represent the four Western elements: earth, air, fire, and water. For example, objects made of ceramic, marble, or stone fall into the "earth" category. Fans that circulate air through your home could represent the element "air." A fireplace, wood stove, or candles symbolize "fire." An aquarium or fountain could bring in the "water" element.

Combine the five Chinese elements in your home.

The Chinese view the elements differently than we do in the West. Feng shui practitioners combine five elements—fire, water, earth, wood, and metal—to produce balance. Include furnishings made of these materials in your home to create a healthy and harmonious living environment. (For more information, see my books *10-Minute Feng Shui* and *10-Minute Clutter Control*.)

Offset too much yang energy with cool colors.

When yang energy predominates, as a result of noise or activity for instance, stress can become problematic. You can counteract too much yang energy in an area by painting or furnishing it with cool yin colors: blue, green, or black.

Balance too much yin energy with warm colors.

When yin energy predominates in an area, due to darkness or cold for instance, lack of vitality or enthusiasm can result. To offset this condition, paint or furnish the space with warm yang colors: red, orange, or yellow.

Place a piece of quartz crystal in your living room window.

Quartz crystal augments whatever it touches. Because chi enters your home through the windows, you can increase its positive effects by placing a chunk of natural quartz crystal on the windowsill where it will catch and amplify sunlight. (Note: Don't use leaded crystal; it doesn't have the same chi-enhancing properties.)

Wash all the mirrors in your home.

Mirrors are a popular feng shui cure with many and diverse uses. One of these is to "double" the effect of whatever a mirror reflects. Dirt, however, diminishes and distorts the reflecting power of a mirror. Clean all your mirrors in your home so they reflect properly and generate health, wealth, and happiness.

Clean out your basement.

The basement symbolizes your subconscious. By cleaning out your basement, you address past conditions or repressed issues that may have been lingering in your subconscious and interfering with your well-being. If this task seems overwhelming, break it down into manageable components. For example, clean only a corner or section of your basement at a time. Sometimes it can be advantageous to clear out your basement—and corresponding subconscious clutter—little by little, so the changes don't occur too rapidly and cause disruption.

Clean out your attic.

The attic represents your mind and spiritual path. Cleaning up clutter in the attic makes room for new ideas and promotes mental clarity. This task, like cleaning your basement, can be broken down into small segments and accomplished over a period of time. That way, it doesn't seem so intimidating and the related personal changes that result can be more easily integrated into your lifestyle.

Get rid of objects that have unpleasant associations for you.

Items that remind you of unpleasant experiences or people you don't like can be a subtle source of annoyance. Instead of letting them trigger negative thoughts and feelings, get rid of these objects.

Rearrange furniture periodically.

To keep your life from becoming static, rearrange the furnishings in your home from time to time. One of the fundamental principles of feng shui states that when you make changes in your home, you spark changes in your life, too. Rearrange furniture in your bedroom to perk up your love life; move furniture in your living room to stimulate friendships. (Tip: To keep changes manageable, move furniture around in one room or area at a time—too much change all at once can prove to be unsettling.)

Clean your fireplace or wood stove.

A dirty fireplace or wood stove is both inefficient and unsafe. It may also be unhealthy, circulating polluted air into your environment. Because one of the main sources of chi is the air you breathe, make sure your fireplace or wood stove is clean and in good working order. In feng shui, the fire element is linked with growth, vigor, enterprise, and creativity. The fire element also stimulates and boosts chi in your environment. On a symbolic level, therefore, an ash-filled fireplace or stove can limit your vitality, enthusiasm, and good luck.

Clear your Health Gua to promote well-being.

In feng shui, the center of your home is connected with your health—it's known as the Health Gua. Clutter or obstacles in this area can lead to physical problems or exacerbate existing conditions. Broken or damaged objects in your Health Gua may symbolize physical impairments—fix them or get rid of them. Keep this area clean and in good repair to encourage the presence of healthful chi and to promote overall well-being. (Tip: Place something in your Health Gua that symbolizes vitality to you, such as a live plant. For more information, see my books *10-Minute Feng Shui* and *10-Minute Clutter Control*.)

Enter each room of your home every day.

Chi can stagnate in an unused room. To activate chi and keep it circulating through your home, enter each room every day. Turn on the lights, play music, water plants, ring a bell, or engage in other activities to keep chi from getting stuck.

Use ceiling fans to keep chi from getting stuck.

Many offices in high-rise and temperature-controlled buildings suffer from stagnant chi because windows can't be opened to allow fresh air to circulate. Ceiling fans help to stir up "stuck" chi and keep it moving freely. If ceiling fans aren't an option, use a small desktop fan to circulate chi through your immediate area.

Close toilet lids and shower curtains.

Chi flows away from your home via drains, especially the toilet. Closing the toilet lid and shower curtain keeps chi from "going down the drain."

Place a small fountain in your office or work area.

The soothing effect of running water helps reduce tension in your workplace, while providing symbolic nourishment to increase your income. The stones in the fountain help stabilize chi and your finances so you don't spend more as you earn more.

Place a piece of amethyst on your night stand.

The soothing vibrations in amethysts can have a calming effect on your nerves and help you rest peacefully. Place a chunk of amethyst on your nightstand to help induce restful sleep and pleasant dreams. Or, if you prefer, wear amethysts to promote feelings of serenity.

Use calming scents in your bedroom.

Vanilla, lavender, and other soothing fragrances can help you relax and sleep better. Put a few drops of essential oil on a handkerchief and keep it near your pillow. Or, burn incense or a scented candle to infuse your bedroom with calming aromas.

Slow the movement of chi down a long hallway.

If your home has a long hallway running from the front door to the back, chi may enter your home but rush right out the back, without circulating properly through the entire living space. To slow the rapid movement of chi in this type of set up, place attractive focal points at intervals along the hall—pictures, plants, furnishings, and so on. Even lights focused to shine at different spots can direct the flow of chi in a more peaceful and auspicious manner. If you wish, install ceiling fans, mobiles, or wind chimes in the hallway to circulate chi into the rooms adjoining it.

Use a negative ionizer.

Electrical equipment and heating systems generate positive ions in your environment, which can produce stress. Install a negative ionizer to counteract the unwanted effects of positive ions.

Clean inside air with an air purifier.

Use an air filtration system or purifier to clear dust, dirt, smoke, and other impurities from the air in your home or workplace. Stagnant chi clings to dust. And because one of the main sources of chi is the air you breathe, clean air is a factor in good health.

Avoid synthetic wall-to-wall carpeting.

Many people experience allergic reactions, breathing problems, headaches, and other problems linked with the chemicals used in the manufacture and installation of wall-to-wall carpets. Whenever possible, use area rugs made of natural materials to prevent unhealthy chemical emissions in your home or workplace.

Visit sacred sites.

Since ancient times, people have traveled to holy places for healing and enlightenment. Many of the world's sacred sites are located in spots where powerful earth chi collects, which is why visiting these sites, and drinking water from holy wells, for instance, can produce positive results. Immersing yourself in the energy fields at sacred sites such as Stonehenge, the Temple Luxor, Teotihuacan, and Lourdes can have a positive effect on your own chi.

Sit *under a tree.*

Trees have long been revered as reservoirs of the life force and conduits between the worlds. According to chi kung philosophy, trees hold a very powerful form of chi that you can tap by sitting under a tree or walking in the woods. The ancient Druids believed trees embodied healing power and wisdom. The Buddha sat beneath a bodhi tree to gain enlightenment. The Norse god Odin hung nine days on the World Tree Yggdrassil to bring the knowledge of the runes to humankind. Sit under a tree, relax, close your eyes, and feel the earth energy flowing up through its roots and trunk. Tune into this earth chi and let it strengthen your own personal chi.

RESOURCES

10-Minute Clutter Control, by Skye Alexander (Gloucester, MA: Fair Winds Press/Rockport Publishers, 2004).

10-Minute Feng Shui, by Skye Alexander (Gloucester, MA: Fair Winds Press/Rockport Publishers, 2002).

The Art of Aromatherapy, by Robert Tisserand (Rochester, VT: Healing Arts Press, 1977).

Awakening Intuition, by Mona Lisa Schulz, M.D., Ph.D. (NY: Three Rivers Press/Crown Publishing Group, 1998).

Body Talk, by Rochelle Gordon (NY: International Rights, Ltd., 1997).

The Complete Family Guide to Alternative Medicine, edited by C. Norman Shealy, M.D., Ph.D. (Shaftesbury, Dorset, England: Element Books, 1996).

A Complete Guide to Chi-Gung, by Daniel Reid (Boston: Shambhala, 2000).

The Complete Illustrated Guide to Chinese Medicine, by Tom Williams, Ph.D. (Shaftesbury, Dorset, England: Element Books, 1996).

The Essential Rumi, translated by Coleman Barks (San Francisco: HarperSanFrancisco, 1995).

Flower Essence Repertory, by Patricia Kaminski and Richard Katz (Nevada City, CA: The Flower Essence Society, 1994).

The Gift: Poems by Hafiz, translated by Daniel Ladinsky (NY: Penguin Arkana, 1999).

The Healing Tones of Crystal Bowls, by Renee Brodie (Vancouver, Canada: Aroma Art Ltd., 1996).

How to Know Higher Worlds, by Rudolf Steiner (Hudson, NY: Anthroposophical Press, 1994).

Magickal Astrology, by Skye Alexander (Franklin Lakes, NJ: New Page Books/Career Press, 2000.)

The New Holistic Herbal, by David Hoffmann (Shaftesbury, Dorset, England: Element Books, 1983).

Planets in Signs, by Skye Alexander (West Chester, PA: Whitford Press/Schiffer Publishing, 1988).

The Power of Now, by Eckhart Tolle (Novato, CA: New World Library, 1999).

Simple Yoga, by Cybele Tomlinson (Berkeley, CA: Conari Press, 2000).

Thorson's Complete Guide to Vitamins and Minerals, by Leonard Mervyn (NY: Thorson's Publishing Group, 1986).

Today's Herbal Health, by Louise Tenney (Pleasant Grove, UT: Woodland Publishing, 1997).

You Can Heal Your Life, by Louise L. Hay (Carlsbad, CA: Hay House, 1984).

ABOUT THE AUTHOR

Skye Alexander is the author of *10-Minute Feng Shui, 10-Minute Clutter Control, 10-Minute Tarot, 10-Minute Crystal Ball, 10-Minute Magic Spells, Magickal Astrology, Planets in Signs,* and the mystery novel *Hidden Agenda.* She coauthored *Your Birthday Sign through Time* and *Love Signs and You.* Her stories and articles have appeared in many magazines and anthologies, and she is a partner in the publishing cooperative Level Best Books. A longtime student of holistic healing and spiritual practices, she lives in Massachusetts with her cat, Domino.